ESP Ideas

Recipes

for teaching

professional

and academic

English

Pilgrims

LONGMAN

Randal Holme

Longman Group UK Limited,
Longman Group Ltd, Edinburgh Gate, Harlow,
Essex CM20 2JE, England
and Associated Companies throughout the world.

This book is produced in association with Pilgrims Language Courses Limited of Canterbury, England.

First published 1996

Set in 10/12pt Cheltenham Book

Printed in Singapore

ISBN 0 582 209773

Text Acknowledgements
We are grateful to Longman Group UK Ltd. for permission to use extracts from *Longman Dictionary of Contemporary English* (1987) and *Longman Dictionary of Business English* (1993).

Illustrations
Cover illustrated by Rosamund Fowler
Illustrations by Kathy Baxendale

Photocopying

A letter from the Series Editors

Dear Teacher,

This series of teachers' resource books has developed from Pilgrims' involvement in running courses for learners of English and for teachers and teacher trainers.

Our aim is to pass on ideas, techniques and practical activities which we know work in the classroom. Our authors, both Pilgrims teachers and like-minded colleagues in other organisations, present accounts of innovative procedures which will broaden the range of options available to teachers working within communicative and humanistic approaches.

We would be very interested to receive your impressions of the series. If you notice any omissions that we ought to rectify in future editions, or if you think of any interesting variations, please let us know. We will be glad to acknowledge all contributions that we are able to use.

Seth Lindstromberg
Series Editor

Mario Rinvolucri
Series Consultant

Pilgrims Language Courses
Canterbury
Kent
CT2 8AP
England

Randal Holme

Randal Holme graduated from Essex University and has done post-graduate study at the Universities of London, York and Essex. He has been involved in EFL, ESOL and ESP as a teacher, teacher trainer and adviser in commercial, academic and school environments in Australia, Europe, Africa and the Middle East. He has produced a wide variety of ELT and ESP teaching materials as well as contributing to several books of teaching activities. He is the author of *Talking Texts* (1991 Longman, in this series). He has also written about literacy and is currently lecturing in English for Academic Purposes and English Language Teaching Methodology at the University of Durham. Present research interests include the role of metaphor in language teaching and techniques for low resource classrooms.

Dedication

To colleagues and students at
Marien N' Gouabi University

Contents

Index of activities

ESP Area Key	EAP = English for Academic Purposes
	EBP = English for Business Purposes
	EOP = English for Occupational Purposes
	EPP = English for Professional Purposes
	ESP = English for Specific Purposes (i.e. this task is multidisciplinary)
	EST = English for Science and Technology

Introduction

WHO THIS BOOK IS FOR

This is not another book that answers the question: 'What is ESP?' It will not debate the question of where General English ends and where ESP begins, let alone question whether the two subjects are really different at all. This book offers some teaching ideas that may be useful for ESP teachers. It will take the view that ESP is not a separate discipline from general EFL or ESOL. It will also suggest that ESP teachers deal with areas of language and skills that English for General Purposes teachers should think about more carefully. This is therefore a book that has something to say to all ELT teachers.

WHAT ESP CAN OFFER GENERAL ENGLISH TEACHERS

One of the less noticed results of an interest in ESP has been to throw a spotlight on some of the neglected themes of language. Such themes as 'calculation' or 'description of systems' are not always linked to specialised needs. Most general English students will find themselves having to describe a system at some point or being confused by large numbers. A secondary school teacher following a general ELT syllabus may also find it rewarding to touch upon the language of maths and science.* Old topics can take new life when looked at through a different language. One can go further. English teachers use enigmas and puzzles to get their students asking questions or simply talking. It is often more stimulating to use the puzzle of new knowledge itself. Students thus acquire language not to learn some new discipline but through the process of studying that discipline itself. One can then talk about learning English *through* Science not *for* Science.

Most academic and professional education attempts to impart knowledge. It is information-centred. The skills that students need to process this knowledge are generally acquired as a by-product of their studies, yet they may be of greater long-term importance. Knowledge is often specific to particular jobs or situations, but skills are something a person can take with them everywhere. They are what enables the individual to cope with new circumstances. For the ELT student, knowledge is the language itself and as such, it can never be totally learnt. The language that the student retains may serve in

---

* Indeed, many secondary-level ELT courses have a pronounced interdisciplinary element in order to fulfil ministry requirements.

one situation but not in another; it is the skills which enable development of new knowledge for new circumstances. This is as true for the General English student as it is for the specialised one. The focus of much ESP on skills and sub-skills has created a useful repository of experience that all language teachers can tap into.

Some ESP teachers try to meet needs which are so specialised that their courses can only be prepared for one person at one time. Such teachers find themselves struggling with subject-matter whose difficulties make them into their student's student. The course becomes a partnership in exploration, with teacher and student supporting each other with their different knowledge. It is inevitable that a book of ESP ideas will have less to say to teachers faced with this kind of assignment, but it can offer a few general principles and suggest ideas for adaptation. The only teachers to whom this book can offer nothing are those who approach language as if it were not a tool for extending the student's reality, but some system where 'how you say it' is somehow detachable from 'what is said'.

Whether we are talking about language or language skills, ESP cannot be shut away in some separate compartment that General English teachers feel unable to enter. ESP teachers may go about their work somewhat differently from their General English counterparts, but it is exactly this difference which can help others to rethink what they do as well.

ENGLISH FOR ACADEMIC PURPOSES

ESP and English for Academic Purposes (EAP) have developed together. Like many teachers, my first experience of teaching specialised language was in a university situation where academic study was the course's 'specific purpose'. According to this interpretation, EAP was a kind of ESP. More recently it has been proposed that EAP deals with a wider content area than could be implied by ESP. EAP is specialised because it has identified particular kinds of skills such as listening and note-taking that students have to master, not because it enables the understanding of legal or engineering terminology. One can then say that ESP can be subsumed by EAP (Jordan, RR, 1992). You could go further still. Many teachers approach language study skills in contexts that are not academic. ESOL teachers in English-medium schools or vocational colleges tackle study skills every day at the lowest levels. They have tapped into another kind of teaching called *English for Study Purposes*. Perhaps this EStP should in turn subsume EAP, because it encompasses something that happens in every kind of educational institution everywhere. Such a line of reasoning risks becoming very unhelpful. One is simply putting boxes round boxes. For my purposes here, an ESP course is one that is given to students who have to specialise in an identifiable area of language or of skills. EAP suggests such an area, although the zone of specialisation is very wide. In short, EAP is wide-angled ESP, but it can also be more narrowly focused. Foundation students decide that they will study sciences and the ESP teacher supports them with a course in Scientific English. Some of the group go on to do biology and their English course can specialise still further. There is no definite point in this process of specialisation where one can say that a student has passed from EAP to ESP or back. All that can be said is that what is taught is determined by the student's needs and that the more specialised these are, the more narrowly focused the English course can be.

ENGLISH FOR OCCUPATIONAL PURPOSES

It could also be argued that EOP and EPP (English for Occupational/ Professional Purposes) courses subsume ESP just as EAP does. However, my own view is that when a teacher states that they are teaching for an objective that suggests they should be concentrating on one group of language topics, skills and genres rather than another, then they are moving into the zone of ESP. EOP is really a statement about the kind of ESP that the teacher is going to engage in. How specific the course actually is depends entirely on its circumstances. An in-company language training course for receptionists is likely to be much more narrowly focused than one for business studies students in a French-medium college. The college course has to be based on some vague projection of what the students may or may not do with English in their future. The in-company course can be based on an analysis of what receptionists actually do with English. However, each course has its specific purpose, however broadly or narrowly focused.

ESP AND GENERAL ENGLISH

It is in the nature of a language syllabus to be selective. The General English syllabus is based on a conception of the kind of reality that the student has to deal with in English. For example, a General English course for teenagers will probably be written around the language-based activities of a stereotypical European teenager. Finding out or even speculating on what these activities are is like taking the first steps towards a needs analysis. Consciously or unconsciously, therefore, all sensible course designers must begin by trying to assess students' specific needs. ESP is simply a narrowing of this needs spectrum.

The ESP process of specialisation should not result in the complete separation of one part of the language from another. One cannot simply hack off pieces of a language or of skills then expect them to exist independently of anything else. Every discipline refers to others and each draws on the same reservoir of language. A science student who comes to grips with the past simple passive through the description of laboratory procedures is unlikely to lock that tense into that context for the rest of their English-speaking life. In the language of diagnosis, the aware medical student will see the larger theme of cause and effect. Teachers and students may prefer to show how a part of the language works by going outside the specialised context that was their starting point. Thus students might learn to describe biological systems by dealing with mechanical ones (Hutchinson/ Waters, 1987, p.116). The ESP course cannot ignore the very obvious point that one language point is often better understood when viewed in varied contexts and situations.

The zone of ESP then, is not divided into a series of independent and mutually-exclusive states. The zone is a confederation of disciplines, skills and teaching techniques. One subject can provide access to another and several may be governed by the same linguistic themes or the same skills issues. This book aims to operate across the confederation.

ADAPTING THE ACTIVITIES TO SUIT YOU

To get the most out of this book, you must treat its ideas as adaptable. I have described some of the activities here as if they were for teachers working in a particular subject area. Often, however, I am only using that subject area to show how the activity works. Other activities, such as those about numbers, may be more closely linked to their subject content, but these often deal with language areas that most ESP teachers will have to touch upon at one time or other.

Experienced cooks know that recipes can be adapted to their own or their customers' taste. The same is true of teaching recipes. You can approach them in either of two ways: as procedures to be implemented as they are, or as ideas around which to improvise.

Some teachers may be worried by a lack of instructions about feeding in lexis or dealing with terminology. Vocabulary teaching itself involves separate activities and several books dealing with these have already been written. Every teacher will have their own ways of presenting the vocabulary for a particular activity and inserting some of my own would merely make the instructions too confusing or too long. The issue of *when* or *how* to teach specialised lexis is more complicated. It leads to the debate about how far the ESP teacher should encroach on the subject teacher's boundaries and whether it is possible to teach the language of a discipline without teaching the discipline itself. This debate becomes sterile because ESP is above all about the specificity of each teaching situation. The question should really be answered on a case by case basis and it depends on the following:

1 the attitudes of the students: how much specialised input they want, how closely they want the ESP teacher to follow the content of their other courses;

2 the knowledge of the ESP teacher about the students' specialisation;

3 the relationship of the ESP teacher to the subject course teachers: whether the ESP teacher confers regularly with subject teachers, how much they teach each other, the extent to which they are jealous of their particular provinces, how closely the ESP teacher can follow students in their other courses.

And these are issues that should be clarified by a sensitive needs analysis.

OVERVIEW OF CHAPTERS

It should already be clear that this is not a subject-specific book. There are no chapters called: 'English for Science and Technology' or 'English for Business,'* The chapters focus on the types of skill or language topic that a career in ESP has seen recur most frequently. The first chapter constructs class activities out of some approaches to needs analysis. The second introduces the very useful concept of *genre*, and proposes a group of teaching techniques called 'genre-switching'. The third chapter suggests approaches to the skill of finding the information that matters. In the fourth, I suggest ways to help students with tasks of giving, understanding and acting upon instructions. The fifth groups together activities that practise the expression of calculation and of related problems. The sixth looks at ways of visually representing data, or describing such visual representations. The seventh chapter turns to the problem of defining and describing a given phenomenon while the eighth gets students to practise the skill of rational argument. In the ninth and final chapter, I propose some ways to help students to function better in meetings and seminars.

* although this information is available in the 'Index of activities'.

CHAPTER 1

Negotiating needs and course content

Needs and ESP are inextricable. Needs cannot be defined simply as the language the student has to acquire. Needs are not only where the students are heading to but also where they are coming from. Defining needs is a kind of navigation through language.

The navigational image is useful but deceptive. Cartographers have a well-developed and recognised system for mapping geographical space, but the language teacher is not so fortunate. There is no agreement about how language should be mapped or even about what exactly it is. Every new way of viewing language demands a new map. The debate is still open as to whether a language-learning curriculum should be defined in structures, speech acts, functions and notions, topics, themes, lexis, skills, mini-skills, tasks, activities, teaching strategies or in varying combinations of these. The choice will be guided not just by how teachers see language, but by how their students have been taught to see it and by the view of the educational system in which they are going to operate. The needs map is not simply a linguistic or even a paralinguistic undertaking. A route is to be charted not just through language, but through the intricacies of different learner behaviours and teaching conditions. The teacher cannot be assumed to be some infinitely adaptable being. The teacher's psychology may itself be something to which at some level the course will have to adapt. Further, the way to go can never be objectively established as the best choice among a set of different possibilities. The 'needs that are established for a particular group of students . . . will be influenced by the ideological perceptions of the analysts' (Robinson P, *ESP Today: A Practitioner's Guide*, (Prentice Hall International, 1991), p.7) and also by the bias with which every individual views their own future. An exact and uncontroversial voyage into language is impossible.

ESP teachers would also be unwise to think that, having decided where to go, they can simply sail on regardless. An EAP teacher may decide that because the class consists of students of electrical engineering their course will be restricted to related content. A few weeks later the students begin to yawn over yet another treatise on electricity then ask: 'We do this all day. Why are we doing it in the English class too?' Evidently these students have a very different view of their needs to that of their teacher. The differences of view make clear how needs themselves are incapable of dogmatic prescription; they are something that is being frequently negotiated between teacher, the student and the class as the course unfolds.

ESP is not just about finding the right course content, it is also about finding the best way to teach for specific needs. An ESP teacher cannot merely select what seems to be the right mix of language and skills then teach it in the way that best fits their preconceptions about how people learn. Learning must be seen as a sociological as well as a psychological issue, related to the question of how people have been taught to learn and how they should best go on learning. ESP teachers may try to introduce changes, but they may also have to make the best of a system as they find it. Some may not like the ideological implications of this. But the question really comes down to making the best use of the time available. When thinking about teaching approaches, they might consider whether they have time for extensive learner training, or perhaps, more to the point, can they afford *not* to retrain the learner? Discovering the tamper-proof features of a learning situation is part of the art of needs analysis.

The following activities are not a teacher's guide to needs analysis. They are about using the tools of the needs analyst to help your students understand what they are doing and why. The activities follow a kind of progression which relates to the activity type and to where it might be inserted in a course. The first activity is about needs sensitisation and ice-breaking. In the second and third, students are asked to look more closely at what their needs are. There is then a shift towards more impressionistic ways of thinking about the same question and towards activities that are also useful for giving the teacher feedback midway through the course.

THE MARRIAGE CONTRACT

Language needs are not a familiar topic for most students. What people want from a marriage *is* something that most people still think about. Here, students approach the less familiar type of need through the more familiar one.

In Class

1 Ask your students to work alone and to decide upon the ten guiding principles of a marriage. They should write down the ten things that they would contract their partner to do in order to create the best possible relationship.
2 Pair off male and female students if possible. Get each pair to prepare a marriage contract of ten articles based on their combined twenty. Say they have fifteen minutes to produce a complete document. If you have a pair of men together, say that they are working out a compromise document that they will present to a woman or vice versa.

1.1

FOCUS
Breaking the ice, introducing the topics of needs and negotiations

LEVEL
Intermediate to advanced

TIME
45–50 minutes

3 Call time and get a student from each pair to read their compromise proposals to the class. Allow discussion to develop.

4 Write the following phrases on one half of the board in the order written below. Change sex and names and simplify the vocabulary as appropriate:

I, Margaret Jonson, have pleasure in offering you a position as ___.
On the terms and conditions set out below
This contract will take effect from _____.
And will continue until_____.
The contract may be prematurely terminated if the conditions are not adhered to
You will undertake to _____ .
               not to_____ .
               that _____ .
This contract is offered subject to the condition that _____.
I have read the above contract and accept the terms and conditions stated
Signed: Date:

5 Ask a student to use these phrases to begin the class marriage contract.

6 Get another student to continue the contract that is appearing on the board. Each student can use their own clauses or repeat those already used. It does not matter if this makes the document contradictory. Repeat the procedure until you get a complete contract.

EXTENSION

7 Tell students that they will now have to negotiate a contract with you. This will include the principles to be followed if you and they are to work together successfully throughout the course. Working alone, each student writes down the ten principles that they want you to follow. It might help to give language or skills parameters, broad headings of achievements or even suggestions such as *Pronunciation, Writing Skills, Telephone Language, Minimal Correction.*

8 Using the marriage contract on the board and their ten principles, each student tries to draw up a contract that they would like you as their teacher to observe.

RATIONALE

Few teachers can predict and teach every genre their students are going to need. When skilled language users want to work in an unfamiliar genre they may look for a model and adapt it to their own needs (Flowerdew J 1993). Here the genre is writing a contract. In the main activity students identify its features in one context then impose them upon another.

THE CLASS CONTRACT

The exercise helps individual students decide the kind of English each wants to learn, then to blend those needs into a common class purpose.

The exercise is also a useful teacher training exercise and can be used as an example of 'loop input' with students using the schema to plot their own training course.

In Class

1 Write the following headings on the board:

   SETTING   SKILLS   GENRE

2 Explain that:
   Setting is where and under what circumstances we use language.
   Skills are how we use language, they are about putting our knowledge to work in different ways.
   Genre is language used for a particular purpose. E.g. We are writing a letter for business or we are welcoming a hotel guest. It refers to a class of 'communicative events' (Swales JM 1990, p. 52) or exchanges. Genre decides the kind of style that we use. (See the introduction to Chapter 2.)

3 Write up the following phrases below the headings in a random order:

   listening   office   computer manuals   contracts
   biology textbooks   reading   airspeak (radio talk between
   pilots or between pilot and ground control)   translating
   workshop   hotel   writing   skimming texts
   commercial correspondence   speaking on an aircraft
   in a lecture theatre   note-taking   welcoming hotel guests

4 Ask a student to come to the board. Get the rest of the class to suggest how this student should group the phrases under the headings. Help only with individual word meanings at this stage.

5 When the student has finished ask them to sit down.

6 Put a cross against any item you think definitely misplaced and ask the class to move it. Remember teachers themselves may not always agree about this. I would do it in the following way:

Setting	*Skills*	*Genre*
hotel	reading	computer manuals
office	writing	biology textbooks
aircraft	speaking	commercial correspondence
lecture theatre	listening	airspeak
workshop	translating	welcoming hotel guests
	note-taking	contracts
	skimming texts	

1.2

FOCUS
Finding out and discussing language needs, negotiating

LEVEL
Lower intermediate to advanced

TIME
120 minutes (two sessions)

7 Draw lines between some of the items as shown above. Ask students what these mean. Get them to realise how, when you are planning a course, one concept influences another. Thus 'the setting' might influence the kind of skills somebody needs which then decides the type of 'genre' they want to use, e.g. the setting *hotel*:

skills   speaking, translating, listening, writing letters and faxes;
genres   welcoming hotel guests, business correspondence.

Make clear that a given skill or genre may not be used in only one 'setting'. For example, 'business correspondence' would have many settings. Equally, a given 'setting' can suggest many different skills and genre. Explain that there is nothing dogmatic about your list.

8 Clean the board but leave the column headings at the top.

9 Ask a student to come to the board.

10 Interview a student about language needs in front of the class, using the three column headings. Get the student at the board to try and complete the columns according to what is said in the interview, e.g.:

You: Where do you think you will use English?
Student: Hm, ah travelling, in hotels, airports, planes.
You: So you will need speaking and listening skills. How about reading or writing?
Student: Not really.
You: Why do you talk to people in hotels?
Student: To get my room and get food, maybe to complain.
You: OK. Getting rooms, getting food, making formal complaints.

11 Form pairs. Ask student A to interview student B in order to draw up B's needs profile using your headings.

12 Students 1 and 2 swap roles. The rest of this activity will probably take place in the second session.

13 Make sure that every student has had a profile drawn up. Bring the class together. Tell them that you cannot create a course for every student, therefore they must hammer their different profiles into one that can be covered in the time available and which represents the interests of the group as a whole. Ask them to imagine that they are going to present you with a contract that will contain everything everybody most wants to cover. Limit the time to about twenty minutes.

14 When the class are ready, sit down with them and ask them to present their course proposals. Tell them what you think is appropriate and what is not. Persuade and do not dictate, accept their arguments if they hold their ground.

EXTENSION

15 After the class, draw up a compromise proposal, adding in an activities (process) column to show how the needs may translate into actual classroom procedure. Try to find more activities than you need or will have time for. Present the proposal during the next session. Ask students to negotiate a selection based on their preferred learning styles.

ACKNOWLEDGEMENTS

'Loop input' is a term devised by Tessa Woodward to describe the type of teacher training approach where ideas are put across and implemented at the same time. Thus trainees will dictate a text about how to do dictations in the ways it suggests as it suggests them. (Woodward T, 1991, CUP).

WHO? WHERE? WHEN? WHAT?
THE CLASS QUESTIONNAIRE

The questionnaire is probably one of the most popular devices for needs analysis. Here the class constructs their own, and so engage in what is itself a useful language practice activity.

In Class

1 Divide the board into four columns with the following headings:

WHO?   WHERE?   WHEN?   WHAT?

2 Give/elicit the following explanations about the headings:

Who: 'Who you will use English with?' this is not just a simple matter of suggesting a few names or occupations. You will want to know about the person's position, relationship to you, nationality and location.

Where: 'Where you will use English?' This is about circumstances, e.g. in an informal, family situation; at work; on the phone.

When: You want to know about student deadlines and perhaps how long you have for your course. You also want to find out whether the course is to train students for a limited encounter with English or a more extensive one.

What: 'What will you want to say or find out?' Here you want to home in on specialisations and on the more general messages the student wants to convey, e.g. talk about business; write essays about legal topics; find out about what customers need.

3 Start to build a detailed class questionnaire on the board by asking students to suggest as many questions for each column as they can. Write down all the questions you have room for, even if they don't appear relevant.

1.3

FOCUS
Finding out student needs, asking and answering *wh*-questions

LEVEL
Lower intermediate to advanced

TIME
50–60 minutes

4 Put the students into pairs. Ask each pair to produce one questionnaire consisting of the twenty most important questions on the board.

5 Pair off students with a different partner. Each student asks their questions then notes down the answers.

6 Bring the class together and ask them to report on their partner's needs either in large groups or to the whole class.

1.4

STUDYING MY CASE

Making case studies enables you to follow the development of a student's needs over a particular period of time. In this activity students observe their own use of language as if they were somebody else. They then report back to the class on what they found out. The activity is for students who are having to use their English every day. It needs two slots on different days and it requires a good deal of introspection and self-observance, so ensure that your students are willing to be self-revealing and self-critical.

In Class

LESSON 1

1 Ask each student to imagine that they are the hero of their own novel. Get them to think about the last twenty-four hours and to visualise themselves as living through that period like the character in a book. They should think about the people they interacted with, where these interactions took place and what happened.

2 After a few minutes' reflection, split the students into pairs and get them to recount their last twenty-four hours to their partner, talking about themselves in the third person.

3 Ask them to observe themselves over the next few days, paying particular attention to their every interaction in English. They should note down the things that they want to say but cannot, both in class and outside. They can use their mother tongue for these notes, but must be ready to attempt some kind of explanation in English, e.g. *I said: 'I want a beer' and the man said something I didn't understand*, or: *I wanted to tell the teacher how to complete the story, but I couldn't get his attention.*

LESSON 2

1 Ask students what language they found they needed but did not have. If they say something unhelpful such as 'everything', then get them to give details about the day's encounters in English. Ask also about the encounters that inadequate English made them shy away from.

2 Write a summary of one encounter on the board, circle it and draw a line across to the right side. Translate it into a teaching point, this could be given as a skill or topic/function/notion, e.g.:

She couldn't ask for beer ⟶ asking for things in pubs
He couldn't get the teacher's attention ⟶ interrupting

3 As you build up a list of teaching points, simply ask the class which they think most important. Leave out those that are a minority interest. Plan your next lessons accordingly.

4 Repeat as the course develops and needs to change direction.

THE TOSIDPAR PROCESS

1.5

The TOSIDPAR approach to course design is an interesting exercise for you to try yourself, but here, the students do it and you listen in.

FOCUS
Making students think about the problems of course design, problem solving

In Class

1 Sketch the plan below on the board. Make all the boxes roughly the same size and shape.

LEVEL
Intermediate to advanced

TIME
50 minutes

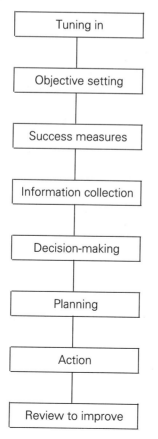

Fig. 1

2 Explain that the diagram represents a way to tackle a problem or reach a decision. You, as a teacher, at the beginning of the course need to decide precisely what your students need. Explain that 'tuning in' is getting to know the problem, finding out the situation and doing reconnaissance, e.g. getting to know your class and finding out what they know.

3 When your students have grasped 'tuning in', ask them what each of the other boxes would mean to you, a teacher trying to solve the problem of their course. Try to elicit the following answers:

Objective setting: the course objectives, where you intend to get the class to, their level at the end of the course.

Success measures: how you will measure the level, how you will know if you have achieved what you intended.

Information collection: testing the class to find out what they know already, or giving them a questionnaire to find out what they want English for.

Decision-making: actually deciding what you want to do in order to achieve the course objectives.

Planning: writing the syllabus, deciding on the activities, tasks, materials that you will adopt and the amount of time that will be needed.

Action: teaching the syllabus, adjusting your techniques according to how the class develops and reacts.

Review to improve: getting feedback to improve the course as it unfolds.

4 Explain that for different problems you can show the relative importance of each stage by drawing its box in a different size. If your problem is 'moving house', the objective is obvious and so 'objective setting' would get only a small box, as would 'tuning in'. Planning is also a lesser item, but information collection (e.g. house-hunting) is complicated so would get a large box. Ask each of the students to redraw the chart showing the relative complexity of the different stages of planning their course with you.

5 Bring the class together and try to establish a class consensus about what the chart should look like, draw it on the board, allow discussion and adjust.

RATIONALE
Although the activity does not tackle course content directly, it encourages students to *talk* about how to tackle it. Such discussions can divulge a lot of useful information about what to put in the course itself.

VARIATIONS
Commercial or technical English students can apply the TOSIDPAR method to problem-solving activities.

1 At step 2 explain TOSIDPAR with an easy example such as 'moving house'.

2 At step 4 give the class a problem in their specialisation, e.g.:
- making a hospital more productive
- transporting Airbus wings from Hatfield (UK) to Toulouse (France)
- providing your company, university or school with the appropriate computer net

Stress that students are not going to solve the problem, but think how to go about it. Bearing this in mind, allow them to ask you for any information they may need:

e.g. *What are the dimensions of the Airbus wings?*

3 Get students into groups of three or four. Each group uses the TOSIDPAR model to analyse the stages of their problem-solving process, then draws the appropriately sized boxes.

4 Try to put one chart on the board, getting students to agree about the correct sizes of the boxes.

ACKNOWLEDGEMENT
I learnt TOSIDPAR from David Francis (1990, pp. 5–30)

CHAPTER 2

Genre-switching

The best known definition of *genre* is 'a class of communicative events with a shared common purpose, examples of which may vary but within allowable constraints' (Swales, 1990, p.46). One problem with this definition is that it does not specify when one 'class of communicative events' can be established as different from another class. For example, was the guide who may have helped you on your last holiday using the genre 'guiding people', 'guiding people in places of interest', 'guiding people in castles' or even, 'guiding people in medieval castles'? Perhaps it's easier to look at the features that constitute the idea of a genre rather than to search for a workable definition. The model below may help.

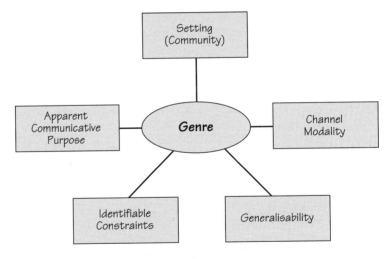

Fig. 2

In order to determine a genre, you need information about setting, that is about the context in which its acts of communication are taking place. You also need to know the channel of the exchange, e.g. phone, fax, letter, spoken message. The genre of 'informal invitations on the phone' is different from that of 'informal written invitations'. You also need to know the apparent purpose. The word *apparent* is useful, since, for example, a guide whose communicative purpose is not really to show you round a castle but to prevent you from seeing the more interesting parts of it, will probably work with the same kind of language as one who is genuinely enthusiastic about explaining the history of the place. The idea of generalisability is essential to establishing class membership. For example, I once ran into a friend on a mountain top in central Turkey. It would not be useful to say that our exchange established the genre of 'meeting old friends on Turkish mountain tops' or probably not even 'meeting old friends on mountain tops'. The genre would be no sooner established than it would become redundant since it is virtually certain that I will never experience anything like this again. It is not even likely that others will use this genre. However, it is very likely that all of us will meet an old friend in unexpected circumstances at some point in time. Therefore a genre called 'unexpected meetings of old friends' could be widely applicable and thus useful to the language learner.

The concept of genre is potentially very useful to ESP teachers because it 'establishes constraints on' the language that can be used 'in terms of content, positioning and form' (Swales, 1990, p. 52). Teaching one genre rather than another makes a course specialised. EST students need the genre of experimental report writing, Commercial English students do not. If you can help your EST students master some of the essential features of the genre of laboratory reports then you are meeting one of their prime language needs.

An ESP teacher can see their aim as helping students to join a particular 'discourse community'. A discourse community is really a group of people who use language in a particular way and for a particular set of purposes. Footballers and their trainers and managers would be a good example. In order to talk about their profession this group will use an identifiable set of genres such as 'giving instructions for taking a free kick near the box', or 'describing positions on the field'. The ESP teacher who could identify and teach the genres would hold the key to helping a foreign footballer join the discourse community of their club.

The central aim of this chapter is to find ways of making the features of given genre clearer and easier to learn. The main tactic is to make the features of genre stand out by imposing them upon a subject matter with which they are not normally associated. One way to observe a given phenomenon better is to put it against an unusual background. A red double-decker bus will stand out more in Tokyo than in London. Parody often bases itself on a disjuncture between style and content. For example, a politician is parodied when somebody uses their pompous style to talk about trivial things. Instead of 'Genre-switching', this chapter could almost be called 'Teaching by Parody'. Such a title would also highlight how genre-switching can be fun. ESP students often complain that their English classes are too similar to their main subject classes. Genre-switching is a way to vary the subject-matter of English classes while keeping them focused on student needs.

The chapter begins with an extreme case of genre-switching, a school story that is rewritten as a laboratory report. In 2.2, students look at business letter style by casting a love letter as a request for employment. 2.3 and 2.4 show how the highly-structured nature of a report can be used to organise an essay. 2.5 highlights an important feature of academic genre called 'metatext'. 2.5 challenges students by thwarting their expectations about genre. 2.7 shows how genre-switching can be used as a dictation technique. 2.8 forces students to talk at cross purposes by using conflicting genres. In 2.9, the switch is from an incorrect literal translation into a correct one. 2.10 considers how different languages and their genres use the same words differently.

2.1

FOCUS
Writing laboratory reports

LEVEL
Lower intermediate

TIME
30 minutes

EXTRAS
Class copies of a text (below)

SCHOOL REPORTS

This activity was first devised for students who were having trouble distinguishing results from conclusions. It also throws a spotlight on other features of report writing.

Explain to the class that there is a genre of 'schoolgirl/boy stories' based on adventures at boarding schools. They were popular with 8–11-year-olds, but are perhaps dated now.

Text

THEFT AT HAGGLEBUSH SCHOOL

Money had disappeared, chocolate and other possessions been taken. Sally was almost certain who was doing it. She knew that Selina Furlingrot had got up in the night just before Suzie Chipper's chocolate had gone. But they had to have proof. Sally decided to set a trap.

Sally and Chipper got a purse and filled it with coins. They left it on the classroom bench during break. Jane Besco and Jill Plump were asked to help. They hid in the class cupboard with Sally while the rest of the class went out.

'Oh, Grotty,' said Chipper, coming up to Selina in the playground. 'There's some chocolate in my desk in class. If you go and get it, half's for you.'

'Ooh, thanks,' Selina said greedily and slipped back to the class.

In the stock cupboard, Sally heard the classroom door open and looked through the keyhole. There was Selina. She went straight to Chipper's desk, took out the chocolate, glanced at the purse then went off to find Chipper. 'She didn't touch it!' The experiment had not had the predicted result. Now there was only one conclusion: 'Selina Furlingrot was not the thief at Hagglebush School.'

In Class

1 Check that your students are familiar with the format, style and subheadings of basic experiment reports, i.e. aim/introduction, apparatus, procedure, results, discussion of results, conclusion.
2 Hand out the text and ask students to read it.
3 Explain that the text is a description of an experiment. Form pairs and ask each pair to prepare a report of the experiment as Sally perceived it. Tell them to make the style of the report as scientific as possible by excluding all unnecessary detail.

4 Call a student to the board. Ask another student to dictate the first section of their report on to the board. Ask the class to correct the style and content. Repeat with a different student for each of the sections. Aim for something like the following:

Aim

The experiment was devised in order to prove the hypothesis: Selina Furlingrot is the thief of Hagglebush school.

Apparatus

a a purse with coins.
b a cupboard
c a bar of chocolate

Procedure

A purse was left on the bench. The suspect was informed there was some chocolate in the room and came back to get it. The suspect's actions were observed by three witnesses hidden in the stock cupboard.

Results

The suspect left the purse on the bench.

Discussion

The results were inconclusive. Although no theft was committed in this instance, the suspect may have been alerted by the behaviour of her colleagues or the circumstances of the case.

Conclusions

The suspect was not a thief.

EXTENSION

5 Ask the class to comment on aspects of their report that make it different from the original text. Highlight those that are firm features of the experiment report.

6 Ask the class to comment on the validity of Sally's experiment. They should spot that the conclusions are not warranted by the results. The more sophisticated may point up such problems as 'observer interference'.

2.2

FOCUS
Writing business
letters

LEVEL
Intermediate to
advanced

TIME
50 minutes

EXTRAS
Class copies of a
letter (below)

THE OFFICE AFFAIR

This exercise tries to make students more aware of some of the features of business letter style by asking them to impose these features on a type of subject normally associated with a very different genre. The exercise may not be suitable for students who might be shocked by using class time to write love letters to imaginary people.

In Class

1 Ask the students to imagine that they are going to propose themselves as somebody's girlfriend, boyfriend or fiancé(e). They should imagine that they are applying for employment in such a post and should list their relevant attributes and qualifications. Warn the class that their lists may become public so that they should not be too intimate!

2 Give each student a copy of the letter (below). Explain that this is a reply, written in business letter style, to somebody who offered themselves as Mrs/Mr Safton's lover. Ask the students to try and write the letter to which this one is a reply, describing their attributes and qualifications in the same kind of style.

3 Circulate and offer editing tips. In particular, suggest ways to make the letter sound more formal.

4 Take back the handout. Collect the students' letters and redistribute them to other students. If possible, give women's letters to men and vice versa. Otherwise appoint men as acting women or vice versa.

5 Tell students to use the style of your handout to reply to the letters received, but to show more interest and to suggest how the attributes of the candidate do or do not meet their requirements.

6 When the students have finished, take the letters in, shuffle and redistribute them.

7 Ask a student to read out one of their letters. Ask the class to listen and decide whether they have an answer or a reply to the letter that has just been read out. If somebody thinks they have, they should read out the relevant letter and the class should discuss whether it does in fact match the letter read out initially.

EXTENSIONS

a Discussion about what you want from a relationship.

b A series of such letters either as homework or as in class leading through interviews, to offer letters and contracts.

WORKSHEET FOR ACTIVITY 2.2

Text

Safton Enterprises
5 Windstock Road
Sandwich
Kent
SNK 32X

4 April 1991

Maynard Bolton
96 Oxford Road
Cirencester
CR7 6KS

Dear Mr/Mrs Bolton,

Thank you for your letter of March 3rd, 1991 enquiring about employment in our company.

I regret that we are now fully staffed and have no opening available for someone of your qualifications and experience. Further, the salary and conditions required would be beyond the resources of a small company such as ours.

We will keep your details on file against the possibility of a change in our staffing requirements. Thank you for your interest in Safton Enterprises.

Yours sincerely,

Patricia/Patrick Safton, Managing Director

2.3

FOCUS
Writing business
letters

LEVEL
Upper
intermediate to
advanced

TIME
50 minutes

EXTRAS
Class copies of an
extract from a
relevant textbook

HEDGING

This is a simple but challenging procedure for aspiring writers and readers of articles or students who want to know how to hedge.

In Class

1 Prepare copies of an extract from a textbook dealing with a subject relevant to the students.
2 Ask students about any differences they may have spotted between the way articles in journals and textbooks are written. Point out that a key difference is that articles tend to hedge. This is because their topic is often state-of-the-art and writers indicate this by drawing tentative conclusions. When knowledge enters textbooks, it is communicated as if it were unquestionably true.
3 Brainstorm for phrases and grammatical ways to hedge and write them on the board: e.g. *one might conclude that, one could postulate, one might be able to show that, at a later date it may be possible that, a result that could emerge, it is thought to be the case that, such a conclusion is somewhat tentative.*

Verbs: *tend to, seem to, appear to, postulate;*
Nouns: *possibility, tendency, likelihood;*
Modals: *may, might, could.*

4 Hand out your text. Ask students to rewrite it as if everything it said were uncertain. Everything said should be hedged. Tell them to exaggerate.
5 Ask students to swap what they have written with a neighbour. They should then try to edit the text as if for publication in an academic journal. They should edit out some, but not all, of the hedges so that the writing that emerges sounds less exaggeratedly tentative and more real.

2.4

LEVEL
Lower
intermediate to
advanced
(depending on the
type of report
used)

TIME
60–90 minutes
(according to
report)

ESSAY TO REPORT AND BACK

Many ESP students tend to over- or under-structure their essays, making them read either like a report or a confusion of thought and fact. In the method shown here, students use the precise structure of an experiment report to help them to organise an essay. They also understand how the seamless essay style contrasts with that of a report.

BEFORE CLASS
Find the description of an experiment (text 1 below). If the description is in report form, be prepared to improvise a mini-lecture around the report. This lecture should miss out subtitles, etc. and could be delivered in a rambling and incoherent way.

In Class

1 Tell the class that you are going to give them a very short lecture. Tell them that they must take notes. They can interrupt you if there is anything they do not understand. Explain the experiment to the class. Try to make the description sound like a slightly confused lecture. You could, for example, give the aim halfway through and talk about some of the conclusions at the beginning.

2 Write the following subheadings down the board with space under each:

Introduction, Aims, Apparatus, Procedure, Results, Discussion of results, Conclusions.

3 Ask the class to imagine that they have just conducted the experiment and must now write a report. Ask them to use their notes to suggest what you should write under the subheadings. Correct as they dictate. Try for the right report style (text 2 below). If science students worry about not having the specifications for the equipment or enough detail, suggest they invent.

4 Ask students to tell you the difference between an essay and a report. Try to elicit how an essay will not have subheadings and that it will read less jerkily. It should be organic, even though it is actually quite tightly structured. Use the analogy of a good gear change. Like a passenger in a car, the reader should not feel the writer changing from *first* to *second*, from *introduction* to *aim*. Use some of text 1 as an example.

5 Ask students to write a mini-essay about the experiment.

6 Hand out the text on which you based your first lecture. Explain that this text could be the type of answer that students are aiming for. However, emphasise that you do not want answers that are exactly the same as this model. Allow them two minutes to read the text then take it away so that they can edit their own essays.

VARIATION

This exercise works with any kind of document whose rigid style and format make the contents of one section more or less predictable from another. I have tried the following switches: business reports to business letters or to business studies essays; application forms to short biographies; series of short subheaded passages from textbooks to experiment reports.

RATIONALE

a The final genre-switch asking students to turn a report into an essay helps them to use the rigid experiment report structure to organise an essay but in a subtler, less visible way.

b Handing out, then taking back, the model text at step six is a useful way for students to rework their own writing round some of the features of the model without allowing them to copy it slavishly.

WORKSHEET FOR ACTIVITY 2.4

Text 1

EXPERIMENT DESCRIPTION

One of the most interesting features of quantum reality is that of observer inter-ference. According to this idea, the observer can effect events by observing them. Such a notion may not seem odd to students of the human sciences, but to physical science people, it still seems strange.

A well-known experiment that illustrates this interference is called the 'Two Slit Experiment'. Here, a stream of photons is emitted from a source. In other words, a torch or laser is switched on. A barrier has been erected in front of the photon source with two slits. These slits allow the photons to pass through. On the other side of the slits, you will find two particle detectors, normally photo multiplier tubes or a wave detector or screen. The extraordinary result is that if the particle detectors are used, the photons travel through one slit and make a click on one of the detectors whereas if the screen is chosen, the photons travel through both slits and leave a wave interference pattern on it. The screen, you see, measures the photons collectively. Therefore, one can conclude that the way one measures light has some effect on the nature of light. When light is measured as particles it is particles. When measured as waves, it consists of waves.

WORKSHEET FOR ACTIVITY 2.4

Text 2

INTRODUCTION

A possible feature of quantum reality is that of observer interference. According to this idea, the observer can effect events by observing them. An experiment was devised to show whether this was the case.

AIM

To test the observer interference hypothesis and to show the dual nature of light.

APPARATUS

Two photon sources or lasers were erected in front of a metal barrier with two slits that could allow the photons to pass through. Two photo multiplier tubes were placed on the other side of the barrier. The tubes were then replaced by a screen.

PROCEDURE

1 The photon sources were switched on then off and the particle detectors were observed.
2 The particle detectors were replaced by the screen and the photon sources were switched on again.

RESULTS

When particle detectors were used, the photons travelled through one slit and registered on one of the detectors. When the screen was chosen, the photons passed through both slits and left a wave interference pattern.

CONCLUSIONS

The experiment showed the dual nature of light. It also revealed how the nature of light changes according to the way it is observed.

2.5

FOCUS
Commenting on a text, writing abstracts or introductions

LEVEL
Upper intermediate to advanced

TIME
40 minutes

EXTRAS
Class copies of any serious newspaper article

A writer's comment on their own text is called the 'metatext' (Mauranen A 1993, pp. 3–22). Metatext is an important feature of many academic genres. One form of metatext is found in the type of introductory paragraph that tells the reader what the rest of the essay or article will be about. Here, it is not text that students comment on but the lesson to come. The activity works best when students know your teaching style quite well and therefore have a fairly solid idea of how your lessons are going to turn out.

In Class

1 Put the class set of newspaper articles on your desk. Remind students how writers of academic papers generally summarise what they are going to say before they say it. Similarly, conference organisers and people giving presentations do the same. Say how some teachers do something similar before each lesson. They say what they are going to do before they start teaching.

2 Ask students to put themselves in your place and to try to tell the class what is about to be taught. What you have already said should give them a fairly clear idea. They can also base their assessment on what they can see on your desk (a pile of texts) and their knowledge of past lessons.

3 Draw a line down the middle of the board. Ask students to tell you their predictions. On the left side of the board, note down their ideas as they give them to you.

4 After they have given you their ideas, try to shape these into an ordered procedure on the right side of the board. Do not worry about getting a lesson plan as such, just a prediction of what you will do.

5 Write the following phrase on the board.

(First) I am going to deal with . . .

Point out that the word in brackets is an adjunct. It is in brackets both because it can be left out entirely and because other adjuncts can be used with the same phrase. Get the class to suggest other adjuncts that could be substituted for this one. They can write them down as they do so, but you should leave the board clear.

6 Write the following phrases on the left side of the board:

(Next) I am going to show   (To conclude) I shall sum up
(Lastly) I will demonstrate   I will (then) examine
(After) I will take as an example (Third) I will deal with
(Second) I will touch upon   The objective of this is
(Finally) I will look at

Ask students to suggest others along the same lines and write these up.

7 Using the lesson prediction on the right side, elicit a formal introduction to the lesson, noting down what students say and correcting it as you do so, e.g. *During this lesson I am going to deal with the topic of writing about your own text. The objective of this lesson will be to make you into more competent authors of academic papers. First I will give you some useful phrases, then examine how they are used. Next, I will distribute the text and ask you to write an introduction to it as if you were the author.*

8 Give your corrected version of what students say to somebody and ask them to dictate it back to the rest of the class who write it down.

EXTENSION

9 Distribute the texts. Tell the students that they are looking at a newspaper article and that this genre does not have the kind of introduction you have just been talking about. Ask students to take the role of the writer and to produce a paragraph in academic style guiding the reader through the article.

RATIONALE

Summarising what you are going to say is an important feature of academic style. It is done in order to guide the reader through what follows, but is also a useful way of getting students to plan their work well. Here, students practise this use of metatext by making an informal lesson introduction sound more formal, a kind of genre-switch.

LETTER FRAMES

Genre is often indicated by very simple cues. Thus the addresses on a letter will often be enough to show that one is dealing with a business letter. Such information can be used to predict a surprising amount of a letter. An interesting exercise can be based on what happens when such predictions fail to come true!

In Class

1 Write the following letter headings on the board:

Wessex Trade Protection
15 Burberry Place
Hardcastle
Wessex W1 HD705

30 January 1993
Sarah Jane Wesley
6 Buddley Close
Hardcastle
Wessex W1 HD213

2.6

FOCUS
Commercial correspondence

LEVEL
Lower intermediate to advanced

TIME
30 minutes

2 Tell the class that these are the headings of a letter. Ask what kind of letter it is. If they say *business, commercial, legal* or even *official*, ask how such a letter would begin. If they say *Dear Sir* or *Madam*, point out that the name is given at the top of the paper, the beginning could therefore be *Dear Ms Wesley* or *Dear Sarah Jane*. Further point out that English-speaking business people move on to first name terms almost immediately after they have met, so you might have *Dear Sarah* etc. Ask for a class decision on how to start. Don't put anything on the board.

3 Ask how the letter will end. If they give you a plausible reply such as:

Yours sincerely,

John Bagworth
Debt Recovery

then write up the beginning and end of the letter but begin a genre-switch. Use a completely inappropriate style. Do not suggest that your students have been wrong. Simply ignore their previous suggestions, e.g.:

My Darling Sarah,
Your ever loving JB

4 Ignore all protests. Continue as if you have written nothing that is in conflict with what the class has suggested. Ask the class what you think a trade protection society could be writing to someone about. Point out the aim of the letter writer (debt recovery). Try to elicit that this is probably an organisation which tries to protect the interests of small tradespeople. Appear to accept various suggestions then continue as follows:

My Darling Sarah,

Leaky Lead Plumbers Invoice PRF 23145

5 Ask students what a trade protection company would be writing about an invoice for. Steer the class to the conclusion that this is probably related to debt recovery. Try to elicit a sensible continuation of the letter, but if they suggest a style similar to 'My Darling Sarah', you could work towards something like:

I was so sad to learn from my dear clients that this invoice was still unpaid on January 29th. Please understand that unless it is paid within two working weeks I may do something that we will both regret bitterly such as dragging you to court. Save yourself from so desperate a measure, settle, I beg you.

6 Elicit a closing message. Switch it to something like:
'Write to me quickly, give me what I desire.'

7 Ask students to search for the language that they might want to keep in a sensible business version of the letter. Underline their suggestions.

8 Ask them to write a sensible version. You might look for something like the following:

Wessex Trade Protection
15 Burberry Place
Hardcastle
Wessex W1 HD705

30 January 1993

Sarah Jane Wesley
6 Buddley Close
Hardcastle
Wessex W1 HD213

Dear Ms Wesley,

Leaky Lead Plumbers Invoice PRF 23145

Our clients, Leaky Lead inform us that payment for this invoice was still out-standing on January 29th 1993. Unless this matter is settled within two working weeks, we shall have no other course but to seek legal redress.

I hope that we will hear from you by return.

Yours sincerely,

VARIATIONS

This will work with any text where the genre is indicated by titles, sub-headings, abstracts, or introductions.

GENRE-SWITCHED DICTATIONS

2.7

FOCUS
Inappropriate
genre style

LEVEL
Intermediate to
advanced

TIME
20–30 minutes

EXTRAS
Class copies of a
text suitable for
dictation that has
been rewritten
with chatty and
inappropriate
interjections. (See
the example text
below)

A creative use of dictation is often an approach well-suited to ESP with its need to train for such activities as taking minutes/letters or lecture quotations. The following is an exercise in recognising the inappropriate and the superfluous then editing it out.

In Class

1 Write the following on the board:

   Abraham University
   Introduction to Computers
   Course Module 2, Input Devices

2 Ask the class to reflect for a minute or two on the genre which the title implies.

3 Tell the class that you are going to dictate a text about the light pen. They are to imagine they have to rewrite this text to go in a textbook. In order to rewrite it they will need to leave out some words, phrases and sentences and include others. They should take down *only* what would appear in a textbook.

4 Read the text once at normal speed. Reread at dictation speed, but still go a little too fast for students to write down everything.

5 Distribute the text and ask students to use it to correct what they have written down, then to help them produce a fair copy that would suit a textbook.

6 A student reads out their fair copy.

Example Text
Now folks let's look at this useful little device called a light pen. A light pen is used to draw on the screen. No, I don't mean you dip it in the ink and draw. You see, it senses the different pulses of light given off by the screen and transmits that information back to the computer. Your computer's clever. It uses that handy bit of information to work out just where the pen is on the screen. Now you move your pen across the screen. Because the computer knows where it is, it can sort of follow it by drawing a line. Clever, eh?

SPLIT GENRES

Students hear people talking to each other in different genres and have to try to get them to use the same one.

In Class

1 Elicit concrete differences between formal and informal registers on the telephone. Students could think about how they would talk to somebody they know well and a business contact that they did not know at all.
2 Read out the dialogue (below) and ask students if they notice anything strange about it. Elicit how the speakers view their relationship differently and are talking to each other in different registers.
3 Distribute the copies of the dialogues and form pairs.
4 The pairs work separately. The A students read Sue in the way written and the Bs change Sam so that he uses Sue's formal register.
5 The As now read Sue in Sam's register and the Bs read Sam without changing him to formal register.
6 Bring the class together. Choose two pairs to read the dialogue; one in Sue's register, the other in Sam's.

EXTENSION

7 Ask students which register would be appropriate to what circumstances. They make up backgrounds of the speakers and of the dialogue to fit one or other register.
8 Ask students if they can think of a set of circumstances that would make this kind of dialogue plausible.
9 Discuss the uses of formal and informal registers in the students' cultures. They should think about whether their languages have more registers than English and how they signal registers linguistically. Do different registers use different vocabulary, word endings, grammar, pronouns or forms of address?

Sam:	Ah, is that you, Sue?
Sue:	Grafton Enterprises, can I help you?
Sam:	Yes, Sue, can you get hold of old Fairweather?
Sue:	John Fairweather, that's extension 343; it's ringing for you now, sir. I'm afraid there's no reply, sir. Can I get him to call you back?
Sam:	Oh damn, look, I've got to go to a wretched meeting, ah, I'll try to get him later.
Sue:	OK sir, thank you for calling Grafton.

2.8

FOCUS
Distinguishing formal and informal ways of speaking

LEVEL
Elementary to upper intermediate

TIME
20 minutes

EXTRAS
Class copies of a relevant dialogue where each participant is using a different style or register from the other participant but in order to do the same kind of thing. (See the example below)

2.9

FOCUS
Formal writing
skills, business
letters

LEVEL
Lower
intermediate to
advanced

TIME
30 minutes

EXTRAS
Class copies of
two literal
translations
(example texts
below)

LITERAL TRANSLATION

Here, students use literal translations as the basis for constructing a
correct English text whose style is appopriate to its genre. **N.B.** This
version is for monolingual classes.

BEFORE CLASS

Prepare literal translations of two different texts from the students'
language where the register sounds very different to what would be
appropriate in English. Try to make the English stylistically inappropriate but grammatically correct. See the requests for a meeting
below.

In Class

1 Form two groups, A/B. Hand out one text to group A and the other
to group B.
2 In their groups, students work alone to produce a version of the
text that is in correct English. They can seek help from other
members of the group only if they are stuck. Circulate and help to
get a correct version.
3 Group A students swap their correct versions with group B students.
4 Students work alone to make a correct, non-literal translation of the
letter into their mother tongue.
5 Give the As the literal translation (text below) that you gave to the
Bs and vice versa. Ask each group to decide how far their translation into their own language reflects the one you made into English.
6 Bring the class together. Discuss the differences between the ways
this genre is approached in their language and in English, e.g.
Modern English begins letters with *Dear*. It does not address people
by job function. The register is less formal. *I have the honour to
inform* = 'I am pleased to tell you.' Letters are signed off *Yours sincerely* or *Yours faithfully* (according to how they are begun). *Best
wishes* is less formal and increasingly common. etc.

EXTENSION

7 Ask students to write a text in similar genre but with a different
subject. Circulate and note down any words and phrases that are
inappropriate and obviously translations. Put the words they are
translated from on the board and suggest English equivalents.

Example Text 1

Sir, the Chancellor of the University of Loubomo,

I have the honour of bringing to your knowledge that Dr. Hasmi, Vice-chancellor of the University of Sind, will be visiting Loubomo from July 5th to July 30th in order to review the progress of our programme of bilateral cooperation.

I would like to seize this occasion to present our compliments.

I pray you, Sir, to accept this expression of our distinguished salutations.

John Hislop
Cultural Attaché

Example Text 2

Sir, the Minister of Secondary Education,

I would like to come close to your esteemed person in order to discuss the new programmes of English of secondary school, here joined, at a time of your convenience.

I would like to send you, Sir, my very high salutations.

John Gorgio
Cultural Attaché

RATIONALE

Students are not asked to make the literal translation themselves because this will involve them in an activity that is time-consuming and uninstructive. The objective here is not really translation at all, but to make clear the way a genre uses language in English. Correcting a literal translation highlights the differences between languages and shows students what they have to learn. Translating back reinforces this learning by reminding students of their mother-tongue equivalents to the English term, but this stage is optional.

VARIATIONS
(for multilingual classes)
1 Use a literal translation from any language that you know and follow steps 1–2.
2 At step 3, divide the board into two halves. Ask students to go through the letter and to tell you every word/phrase that they have changed and what they have changed it to. Write new phrases on the right-hand side of the board and correct as necessary.
3 Ask each student to copy the words/phrases on the right side of the board.

2.10

FOCUS
Vocabulary
development/
usage

LEVEL
Intermediate to
advanced

TIME
30 minutes

EXTRAS
A bilingual
dictionary for
every mother
tongue in your
class

BETWEEN WORDS

A given subject may use general vocabulary in a specialised way. Economists will talk about economic *development* and marketing people about product *development*. *Development* means something different in each of these contexts. However, not all languages will use their most common equivalent for *development* in the same way. This exercise helps students to understand the extent to which they can and cannot shift a given word from one context to another.

BEFORE CLASS

Decide on a word or words that you think will be useful for your students' specialisations but which also occur frequently in other contexts. You are looking for subtechnical rather than technical terminology.

e.g. *develop, expand, revolution, culture, element, item, reflection, subject, frontier, organic, solution, force, source, capital, budget, function, radical, fertile, core.*

In Class

1 Put students into mother-tongue groups, e.g. Japanese with Japanese, French with French etc. Students who are the only speaker of a given mother tongue in the class must sit alone. Groups should have no more than four students.

2 Give students one of your words. Ask students to look it up, to write down the first mother-tongue equivalent they see, then to close their dictionaries.

3 Explain how a given word can be used in different contexts and/or disciplines to mean different things. Give them the example: *Changing the corporate culture* v. *They have no culture* and explain that here the difference is quite great. Then suggest: *economic development* v. *materials development* where the word meanings are closer but nevertheless different in that they refer to very different types of process. Ask students to work in their own language and to write sentences showing the many ways the translation of the word you have given them is used. Next, ask them to go to different forms of the same word. e.g. for *develop*: *under-developed* has acquired a pejorative and negative meaning, we talk instead of *developing* countries.

4 In turn, students try to read out a translation of one of their sentences. If it makes sense with the word you're focusing on, put it on the board. If it doesn't, leave it off.

5 If you can think of useful ways to use the word that students have not come up with, add example sentences. Ask students to think if your sentences make sense in their languages as well. Discuss to what extent the multi-uses of words are metaphorical. How easily do words travel from one discipline to another? Consider these words uses in: Business, Science and Technology, Everyday life, Economics, the Arts.

6 Consider computer/word-processing terms such as: *file, mouse, application, paste-board, bullet, windows, cells*.

CHAPTER 3

Homing in

During my first days as a student in a direct method Spanish class, I sometimes had the feeling that I was manipulating symbols that had been separated from what they represented. Language seemed opaque, its purpose was not to uncover reality but to obscure it. Communicative methodology stresses the contrary. Language is above all a message-bearing medium. ESP teachers must perhaps go one step further still. They do not see English as a subject in itself, they teach English for something else. The activities in this chapter are about helping your students to use English to explore that 'something else' and to *home in* only on the knowledge they need.

Nobody bothers to understand, let alone to retain, all the messages with which a language surrounds them. People have to home in on the messages that are important and disregard those that are not. This 'homing in' is crucial both to study and to professional life. Students need to develop ways of understanding and remembering the important points of a given class or lecture. Professional people have to identify quickly then grasp what is important in a presentation or document.

Information transfer activities are a well-tried way to get students to search texts or tapes for crucial information then to express it in another format. Activity 3.1 is an interactive version of this. 3.2, 3.3 and 3.4 help students with the skill of note-taking and are based on the principle that good notes reflect an ability to understand the important points in a given lecture or presentation. 3.5 switches the emphasis to the more complex task of summarising a meeting or seminar.

INTERACTIVE INFORMATION TRANSFER

3.1

FOCUS
Information transfer, profit and loss, accounting

LEVEL
Elementary to advanced, according to text and table used

TIME
30 minutes

EXTRAS
½ class sets of a text and of a table

In this exercise each partner has information that the other needs and both have a text to complete. The activity will reward you for the considerable time needed for preparation.

BEFORE CLASS
You will need one text and a table that illustrate each other. Remove some key words or facts from the text, (ones also given in the table) and some from the table (ones also given in the text). Do not remove the same item from both the text and table. (See the example below.)

In Class

1 Form pairs. Give As a copy of the table and Bs a copy of the text.
2 Tell As and Bs to sit back-to-back and not to look at each others' papers.
3 Tell As that they must complete the table and Bs the text. B will begin by reading the text. They should stop if asked to by A and repeat numbers or sentences as required. When B comes to a gap in the text, they should hum and wait until student A helps them to complete it by consulting their table.
4 When a pair has finished, get them to go through table and text together in order to sort out any problems.

EXTENSION
5 Students put the texts away. One student starts explaining the table. Indicate the next student who carries on the explanation from exactly where you left off.

ACKNOWLEDGEMENT
The trading and profit and loss account comes from Knott, G 1991, p. 16.

RATIONALE
Most information transfer activities go from text to table or table to text. By going both ways at once this activity keeps both partners involved and makes them use a wider variety of skills.

Example Text and Table for Activity 3.1

PROFIT AND LOSS

Right, I'd just like to take as an example the trading and profit and _____ for Western Shield for the year to March 31, 1991. This way we can all understand what we're talking about. Sales were strong at 2m. The cost of sales was kept to 1,400,000. Now it should be quite obvious that you get the Gross profit by deducting _____ _____ which gives you a respectable _____.

Then to go into more detail: we'll discuss the net trading profit. As you can see, we have to take into account administration expenses at 80,000, selling and distribution expenses of 130,000 and of course – always a sore point for some – the directors' fees and salaries at 40,000. Lastly, we have to pay back the bank so there's the _____. Now, how do we calculate net trading profit? Well, you have to _____ _____ which gives you a round _____.

So, we move on down to 'profit for the year retained' which is the money our company actually gets to keep. First, we have to deduct what we give to the government, or what we call _____. In this case it comes to _____. Next, we can't forget our shareholders. The shareholders' profit is calculated by _____ which gives us _____. Then we have to pay them a dividend of ten thousand for the year and we get the profit for the year retained by deducting that from the shareholders' profit.

Western Shield
Trading and Profit and Loss Account for the year to 31 March

	£000
Sales	
Cost of sales	
Gross profit	600
Management expenses	
Selling and distribution expenses	
Directors' fees and salaries	
Interest on overdrafts and loans	6
Net trading profit	344
Corporation tax	172
Shareholders' profit	172
Dividend paid	10
Profit for the year retained	

MUDDLED TALK

Here, students use notes to separate two jumbled talks. The success of the exercise very much depends on how carefully you select your texts. The examples given are roughly intermediate level in themselves but are made more difficult by the fact that they are in similar subject areas. A greater subject contrast will make the task easier.

BEFORE CLASS

You need two texts that can form the basis of five 10-minute talks in two areas of interest to students. Note places in the texts where you will switch from one text to the other during your talks. Mark these places in the margins with numbers so that you can switch back from one text to where you left off in the other without pausing.

e.g. In the following text A you start at '1' then stop at '2', begin text B at '1' stop at '2', restart 'A' at '2', continue to '3' then go back to B at 2.

Text A

1 Rotary drilling is the most common drilling method. In this method two actions take place together.
2 The drill is pushed downwards. At the same time, it is also rotated or turned. Consequently the *drilling bit* cuts into rock.
   Rotary drilling is performed from a drilling rig. Diesel engines supply power to the rotary machine or table.
3 This is located on the derrick floor above the well. (etc.)

Coleman, 1980, p. 24.

Text B

1 When distillation is complete, a range of fractions is available. From these fractions, many useful products can be obtained. Some products such as aromatics or petroleum coke, are obtained only after *chemical conversion*.
2 Chemical conversion also produces further amounts of fractions such as gasoline.
3 The processes of chemical conversion change the size, structure or shape of hydrocarbon molecules. (etc.)

Coleman, 1980, p. 18.

In Class

1 Say that you are going to give two short talks on different subjects at the same time. Ask students to take notes as if they were attending one lecture on the same subject. They divide their page into two, vertically, and take notes for each talk in separate columns.
2 Begin talk A, switch back in and out of talk B as planned. Try to do more than just read. Add comments and questions such as: *Do you understand? Is that clear? Right*, etc. Also add some extended anecdotes, for example, *Now when I was drilling for Shell in Balikpan*, etc.

3.2

FOCUS
Listening comprehension, note-taking

LEVEL
Intermediate to advanced

TIME
40–50 minutes, according to text length

EXTRAS
Two texts

Use your improvisations to hide the switches from one text to another, e.g.:

> *There we were in the middle of Balikpan, without a diesel to power the rig, yes, as I said, it is through the process of chemical conversion.*

3 Bring a student to the board and ask them to draw a line down the middle. Call one half of the board 'Talk 1' and the other 'Talk 2'. Ask the class to dictate notes that they think belong to 'talk 1' and notes that belong to 'talk 2'. Discuss the result and ask if they want to swap any notes over.

4 Give the two talks again, but one after the other, while students take notes again.

5 Ask students to review the board notes and to decide whether they want to make any further changes or additions.

EXTENSION

6 Assign each student one set of notes and ask them to produce a written summary of one of the talks.

RATIONALE

a Good notes will help students to separate the subjects in retrospect even if they do not fully understand what is going on when they hear the talks. How well students make the separation will depend on how good their notes are.

b Giving students a second chance to get their notes right helps them to understand what they should be aiming for when you repeat the activity.

3.3

FOCUS
Listening
comprehension
and note-taking

LEVEL
Lower
intermediate to
advanced

TIME
30–40 minutes,
according to the
length of the talk

THE SHEEP FROM THE GOATS

Successful note-taking depends on finding what is important in a talk and you writing notes that help you remember what you didn't focus on. This exercise helps students to do just that.

BEFORE CLASS
Prepare a 10–15 minute talk on a relevant topic or select a text around which you will be able to improvise. In either case, include a lot of irrelevant information, anecdotes and invitations for questions. This activity requires an articulate teacher!

In Class

1 Form two groups: the 'sheep' and the 'goats'.

2 Tell the sheep that they must make notes on everything that is important in your talk and the goats on everything that sounds like padding.

3 Start talking and waffle away.

4 Divide the board into two columns. Title one column 'sheep meat' and the other 'goat meat'. Ask a sheep student to contribute an important note for the 'sheep meat' column. Then goat students to contribute an unimportant one for 'goat meat'. Write what you are told without allowing discussion. Continue eliciting contributions.

5 When you have complete columns, ask students if there is anything they would like to shift from one column to the other, mark the items with arrows. Allow discussion.

6 Review the notes in the 'sheep meat' column. Suggest ways to make them more concise, accurate and complete.

MINUTE MERGING

Here, students use notes to put together the minutes of a meeting.

BEFORE CLASS
Prepare an agenda for a class meeting that you will chair, on an issue of interest to everyone that will arouse some difference of opinion.

In Class

1 Pair off your students. Say that every student must listen carefully to what their partner says during the next activity and take notes.

2 Set up a meeting on any topic of interest to the class. Issues affecting their daily life, such as school facilities or courses, work best. Distribute the agenda to the class so that they have the issues in front of them.

3 Take the role of chairperson. Keep to the agenda. Move the meeting along at a good pace and try to get everybody to contribute by asking for opinions.

4 Close the meeting after about twenty minutes. Appoint a class secretary and ask the class to use their notes on what their partner said to help the secretary to construct the minutes of the meeting. Insist that the minute-taker's opinion is what counts and the person who spoke has no say in how their views were recorded.

5 Read the minutes back to the class. Ask students to say whether they think the minutes are an accurate reflection of what they said.

3.4

FOCUS
Note-taking, listening comprehension, summary writing

LEVEL
Intermediate to advanced

TIME
50 minutes

3.5

FOCUS
Understanding meetings

LEVEL
Intermediate to advanced

TIME
60 minutes

THE HIDDEN AGENDA

Here, students try to determine the agenda of a meeting they have just had.

BEFORE CLASS

1 Construct the agenda for a meeting of the students in your class. Choose a topic that you think will interest them. As in 3.4, something that relates closely to their lives as students is generally most involving for all. (See the example below.)
2 Select a student as chairperson and brief them on this agenda. If possible, go for somebody who has had some experience in steering meetings. Tell them they will steer a meeting that covers each item. Say they will have only 30 minutes to produce a list of recommendations covering everything on the list. Ask them to try to elicit contributions from the weaker or shyer members by putting more questions to them directly. Make sure that the chairperson does not show the agenda to anybody else in the class or tell them anything about it.

In Class

1 Tell the class that they are going to have a meeting lasting 30 minutes. Arrange the tables accordingly. Let the chairperson take over. Make notes about errors/especially apt turns of phrase for later. Do not intervene.
2 When time is up, get the students into pairs. Ask each pair to reconstruct the agenda of the meeting and to write a legible version on a separate paper. Stress that you do not want minutes, just what was discussed in what order. At the same time, the chairperson should write a list of the important points raised at the meeting and a list of any decisions taken or recommendations made.
3 Get the pairs to swap agendas. Ask each pair to put action points decided by the meeting (if any) for each item, e.g.:

Canteen   The cook should not try dishes that he or she cannot do (e.g. spaghetti).

4 Bring the class together. Bring the ex-chairperson to the board. Get the class to try to agree on what the agenda really was and what the action points were. The ex-chairperson will write what the students say on the board without adding anything of their own. The chair's role is to sort out disputes, not to impose an opinion.
5 Give students the agenda and ask them if they think this was what they really discussed.

Example Agenda

Meeting to draw up a list of improvements in the running of
_____ school/college/university.

1 Possible educational improvements
   1.1 Teaching methods
   1.2 Teachers' working practices – punctuality, dress, correction of work etc.
   1.3 Course content
   1.4 Examinations/testing
   1.5 Self-access materials, availability of appropriate materials, written, recorded (video/audio)

2 Out-of-class improvements
   2.1 Social programmes
   2.2 Catering
   2.3 Accommodation (if appropriate)
   2.4 Visits (if appropriate)
   2.5 Extra curricular programmes – talks, drama, films etc.

CHAPTER 4

What to do and how to do it

There are two basic types of instruction. The first type involves telling people *what* or *what not* to do and can mean using no more than simple imperatives. *Stand up, don't open the door* etc. The second type is about telling people *how* or *how not* to do something. It can range from a very simple explanation of how to get to somebody's office, through the question of how to undertake a particular assignment and on to servicing instructions in a manual for complex machinery. The relevance of both topics to ESP is not hard to see. Almost immediately, EAP teachers will need to be sure that their students can cope with classroom or laboratory instructions etc. Both EAP and EOP students are likely to need to interpret manuals or other 'how to' documents. Any working life will entail periods of undergoing or leading induction into new work practices or positions. Most people are readers of instructional manuals. Clearly then, instructions are another topic about which ESP teachers have something to tell the world of ELT in general.

The beginning of this chapter deals with the 'what to do' type of instructions. 4.1 borrows from the TPR (Total Physical Response) procedure of having students show understanding by making physical responses. 4.2 looks at the crucial area of understanding exam instructions. 4.3 combines 'how to' and 'what to' instructions in a teacher-friendly version of an 'assembly exercise'. 4.4 is a computer related exercise that tackles 'How to' and 'What to' instructions together. Computer operators often give instructions which the computer carries out. If the instructions are incorrect the operator generally gets feedback fast. Computers are machines that have to be told what to do and how to do it. The final activities 4.5 and 4.6, use recipes in both their culinary and ELT form.

BE CAREFUL!

Exercises dealing with dangerous workshops or laboratories and untidy offices abound in wide-angled ESP courses. They are almost always used to teach the language of instructions or advice. This activity brings the subject to life and lets the students adapt the challenge to their level.

BEFORE CLASS

Imagine an untidy office with a variety of health and safety hazards. Fit your mental picture into a space the size of the classroom. Draw a sketch if it helps you.

In Class

1 Ask students to imagine a dangerous and untidy office. The office can be outrageously disorganised with, for example, machinery on the floor, papers overflowing from the filing cabinet, exposed wiring, broken fittings, worn carpets etc. More mundanely, it could have such hazards as bad lighting, uncomfortable seats, greenhouse-like architecture, depressing colour scheme and noise. Ask students to supply more hazards and list them.
2 Tell students to imagine that their classroom is an untidy and disorganised office. Sketch a plan of the class on the board showing only walls, doors and windows and ask the class to copy it.
3 Send out the student who is sitting furthest from the door.
4 Tell the student outside to come back in. After they've taken a few paces shout: *Stop! Watch the wire!* Tell the class that there is a wire connected to a computer at the student's foot. Draw in a wire at approximately the place where the student is. Tell the student to change direction and let them take another step. Stop them again on account of another hazard. Get the students to draw it on their plans. Repeat with one or two more hazards. Then let that student go back to their place.
5 Send another student to the door. In turn, different members of the class guide them round a hazard, while everybody draws it on to their plan. Repeat with other students until the class runs out of ideas. The class thus build up a plan that potentially includes ideas from everybody.
6 Ask the class to look at their plans and tell you what you should or should not do to make the office safe.

EXTENSION 1

7 Students write an inspector's report using the following headings: *Description of the premises, Hazards and defects, Action points.* Insist on numbered paragraphs and subparagraphs.

4.1

FOCUS
Giving instructions and advice, describing an office or workplace

LEVEL
Elementary to upper intermediate

TIME
20 minutes

EXTENSION 2

8 Use the report as the basis of a role play between two students. Student A is the inspector, student B a very ignorant office manager. The manager points to something listed as a hazard and asks 'why'. The inspector answers.

VARIATION
Depending on students' specialities the setting can be a laboratory, ship, workshop, aeroplane, barn, farm etc.

4.2

EXAM INSTRUCTIONS

FOCUS
Writing and understanding examination instructions

LEVEL
Intermediate to advanced

TIME
30 minutes

EXTRAS
Class copies of the exam instructions and of the questions on separate papers

Misunderstanding or ignoring exam question instructions and rubrics has brought down many otherwise capable students. One way to get yours to pay closer attention to instructions is to get them to write instructions themselves. Doing this kind of activity can also help *you* with writing clear instructions for the tests you write yourself.

BEFORE CLASS
1 Find or write an examination or test question of the kind that needs instructions to tell the student how to proceed. ELT exams often provide the best material here.
(See the example instructions below)
2 Separate the instructions and the example from the question itself.

In Class

1 Divide the class into groups. Give group A the question and the accompanying example of how to answer it. Give group B the instructions.
2 Group B students work alone and, using any available resources, try to write an example and a question. Group A students try to deduce the instructions and to write them down.
3 When the As are finished, tell the Bs to finish also. One A student dictates their instructions while you write on the board. Then one B student dictates their question.
4 Ask both the groups if they would like to correct or refine what is on the board. Discuss suggestions and steer the class to those that are correct.
5 When you have a correct version on the board, distribute both your sample questions and instructions and allow a minute or two for students to make any final revisions.

EXTENSION
6 Repeat with another type of question, allowing As and Bs to swap roles.

Example Instructions and Question

In the following text, a word is missing from each line. Mark where the word is missing in the way shown in the example then, on the line provided, write in a word that fits the context at the end of the line. Note that in order to get full marks for this question you must mark and write.

e.g. The insulator is efficient   _____

It wrong to think that insulators   _____
keep the cold. It is not possible   _____
to cold to anywhere, only heat   _____
can move. Insulators the heat   _____
in, not the out   _____

VARIATIONS
a
1 Work with the type of exam which assumes students know how to answer the questions (i.e. there are no examples of how to answer) but which lets students choose which questions to answer.

   e.g. Time allowed: 3 hours.
   Answer one question from each section. You are advised to divide your time between the questions equally. Make sure that you do not spend too long on any one question.

2 Distribute copies of the exam with the instructions whited out.
3 Ask students to use a mixture of guesswork and judgement to mark the questions that they think they would have to answer in order to pass the exam. Where they feel they have a choice, they can mark questions that they think they can do best.
4 Check students' understanding of the questions by asking each to give a quick explanation of how they would answer one of the questions they have marked. Don't labour this, you are not dealing with how to answer questions so much as whether they are understood in the first place.
5 Write the instructions on the board. Ask students to read them and to think again about what they would answer.
6 Ask the students how close they were to the truth about what to answer in the exam.

b
For a technical, scientific or commercial process: find a description of the process then get students to write instructions for carrying it out.

4.3

FOCUS
Instructions for
setting up
experiments, the
'apparatus stage'
in experiment
reports

LEVEL
Elementary to
intermediate

TIME
30 minutes

EXTRAS
A diagram

THE SUM OF ITS PARTS

Many teachers may have tried 'assembly activities' where students on one side of the room use paper, card, Meccano or Lego to put together a model according to instructions received from students on the other side of the room. The following activity elicits the same kind of language but with much less fuss.

BEFORE CLASS
Find a diagram of either the apparatus for an experiment or of a machine. The diagram should have clear distinguishable parts. The apparatus should be familiar to the students. Make sure that you can identify the parts by name. The following works well with elementary students:

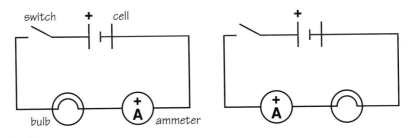

Fig. 3
(Based on Stone, 1993 p.104)

In Class

1 Say the name of a part in your diagram and ask the students to make a quick diagrammatic sketch. Do not tell the class what system this part belongs to. Repeat with all the other important parts of the diagram. Parts used two or more times can have the appropriate number put under them.

2 Write the title of the experiment or the name of the apparatus on the board, e.g.:

   An experiment to show that current is not lost in a circuit.

3 By turns, students tell you how to set up a part of the apparatus while you sketch the relevant part of the apparatus diagram on the board. Insist on language related to setting up the apparatus not to the action of drawing.

   e.g.   Not: *Draw a line showing a wire from the positive terminal of the cell to the switch.*
   But: *Take the first cell. Connect the positive terminal to the first switch.*

   If you do not get the English you want, wait until you do.

4 When your diagram is complete, ask students to disassemble the apparatus by giving you instructions one by one. Rub out the relevant part as you go.

e.g.   A students says: Take the first cell. Disconnect the positive terminal from the first switch.
The teacher rubs out the line joining the diagram of the positive terminal to that of the first switch.

EXTENSION

5 Ask students to write a paragraph describing the apparatus as if for the apparatus section of an experiment report. They can draw diagrams if required.

e.g.   Two circuits were set up (see figs. x and y). In the first, a switch was connected to the cell, a bulb to the other side of the switch and an ammeter to the bulb. In the second, the ammeter was between the bulb and switch.

COMPUTER TALK

4.4

Here, students instruct each other in how to use well-known business applications programs.

BEFORE CLASS

Decide on at least three applications for the software you have installed. Make sure that manuals and machines will be available to class members. Three possible applications are:

1 Word processing Using a macro to head fax messages for a company. The macro should contain: sender's name, position, company, company address, fax and phone numbers; automatic date; slots for receiver's name, company, address etc. The headings should be as clear and attractive as possible.

2 Spreadsheets Using a spreadsheet to record/calculate the weekly profit and loss account for a small shop. The spreadsheet records takings, outgoings, VAT at 17.5 per cent, overheads (rent/electricity) and pre-tax profit/loss.

3 Databases Using a database in a library to record book loans. The records should show the author, title, publisher and location (in the library) of the book as well as any borrower's identity.

In Class

STAGE 1

1 Divide the class into three groups. Give a different application to each group.

2 Ask them to go away and use the manuals and the computer to produce idiot-proof written instructions for the topic.

e.g.   You will see a grid on your screen. Move the cursor to the point A1 using the arrow keys.
Type in: 'Corner Shop Accounts'.
(etc.)

FOCUS
Written and spoken instructions

LEVEL
Lower intermediate to advanced

TIME
Stage 1: 20 minutes + homework time according to subject
Stage 2: 10 minutes + homework time
Stage 3: 30 + minutes

EXTRAS
Access to a computer with business applications software installed. The students should not know the software well. Software manuals

STAGE 2

3 Form groups of three. Tell each group that they will go away to instruct each other in how to accomplish their applications.

A has written instructions for setting up a macro. B and C try to carry out A's instructions on a computer. A watches and tries to explain any problems. A tries not to touch the machine.

STAGE 3

4 Take in the instructions and discuss any problems or defects.

VARIATION

Authoring Software Many teachers with CALL labs use authoring software to write exercises for their students. Ask students to write exercises for each other.

STAGE 1

1 Check that your computers are equipped with relevant CALL authoring software.
2 Form one group of three students. Call them the teachers, give them the software manual and ask them to prepare a simple CALL exercise based on a relevant text for the next week's lesson.

STAGE 2

3 Ask someone in the class to try to do the exercise while the rest of the class observe. (You can do this either by gathering the class round one computer or by having everybody observe what happens on one computer through different terminals in a network.)
4 Form three groups. Assign one of the three students from the 'teachers' group of three to each group.
5 Cluster each group round one computer and have each group decide on a similar exercise they want to construct. Since the exercise will follow the same pattern, this may mean simply selecting a relevant text.
6 Ask each 'teacher' to tell their group how to program their chosen exercise. The teachers should keep their hands off the keyboards at all times.
7 Each group does the exercises of the other two.

TOO MANY COOKS

This activity is not a digression into ECP or English for Culinary Purposes! However, recipes *are* process instructions and are useful to any teacher covering instructional language in whatever subject area.

In Class

1 Dictate a sample recipe i.e. ingredients followed by instructions.
2 Get a weaker student to read back the dictation. Correct any language mistakes that can be picked up from the reading. Leave spelling mistakes for later.
3 Ask each student to study the format and style of the recipe that they have taken down and to use it as a model to write one recipe of their own. Try to get a balance between first, second courses and desserts. If a student says, *I can't cook* just tell them to write idiot-proof instructions for frying an egg.
4 Walk round, observe and correct the dictations done in step 1 while students are writing.
5 Redistribute the recipes written by the students in step 4. Ask each student to imagine they have followed the recipe they have just been given and to write a report about what happened under the headings; 'Procedure', 'Results', 'Conclusions'. If you are dealing with EOP students, you can add: 'Action Points'. Explain that procedure should be a description of what they did and that it should be written in a clear impersonal style, using the passive voice where appropriate. The difference between results and conclusions often causes problems. Illustrate this with the following examples:

Elementary/lower intermediate
Results: Tough meat in a good sauce.
Conclusions: We could not eat much.

Upper intermediate/advanced
Results: A curious gelatinous concoction.
Conclusions: The experiment did not produce an edible dish.

The heading 'Action Points' is there to give the student an opportunity to improve the recipe. This heading is a feature of business and civil service reports, e.g. *Action Point: Add more salt.*

RATIONALE
At step 3 students identify the features of the genre then try to imitate them. This is an important skill for any foreign language user. Step 5 makes the impersonal features of the report genre stand out by imposing them on an untypical subject matter. Those interested in this technique should look at Chapter 2: Genre-switching.

4.5

FOCUS
Procedure instructions

LEVEL
Elementary to advanced

TIME
According to recipe and cut-off point

EXTRAS
A cooking recipe

4.6

FOCUS
Instructions

LEVEL
Intermediate to
advanced

TIME
Variable
according to
recipe

EXTRAS
Class copies of
the recipe given
to the pair of
students before
the class, class
copies of another
straightforward
language teaching
'recipe' (not the
one that your
students have
prepared to use)

ELT RECIPES

Here, students instruct each other in order to set up class activities.

BEFORE CLASS

1 Choose a short language-teaching recipe suitable for your class (possibly from this book!).
2 Choose a pair of students who are not afraid of making mistakes or being in the limelight.
3 Take the pair aside. Explain any likely points of difficulty in the recipe. Then ask the two students to take it home and study it. Say that they will teach the class the next day. Point out that you are not expecting them to be a 'teacher' in the full sense, only to give instructions to the class to tell them what to do. Tell them that if they have problems getting the other students to understand the instructions in English they should use their mother tongue (if the class is monolingual). Remind the pair that you will be on hand to help.

In Class

1 Tell the class that students A and B are going to give a lesson today.
2 Ask A and B to begin with one taking the main teaching role and the other assisting. If you have to intervene, try to do so by talking quietly to different students from the back. Avoid taking over the class. Thank the students.
3 After the lesson, distribute copies of the teaching recipe that has not been taught and give them 5–10 minutes to study it.
4 Form pairs. Ask each pair to think back over their recent lesson and imagine that they must give instructions to another teacher about how to lead that lesson. They should write out a recipe using the same kind of register and format as the one that they have in hand. At the same time, ask the pair who gave the lesson to try to rewrite from memory and to incorporate any changes they would like to make or which were inadvertently made.
5 As students finish, give them a copy of the recipe on which the first part of the lesson was based. Ask them to compare it with their own reconstruction. (It is sobering to find out how much a teacher's and a student's perception of a class procedure can vary.)

RATIONALE

I began doing this exercise with teacher trainees, many of whom have been as much in need of language improvement as of methodology. Then it occurred to me that something which provided language practice for trainees could do the same for students in general. Additionally, it seemed that this could encourage them to think more carefully about how they were being taught and to take more control of their learning.

CHAPTER 5

Words that add up

Calculation can be treated both as a language topic and as a skill. Different students will demand different forms of treatment. Some may be highly numerate in their own languages and will have no trouble adapting this skill into a foreign language. Others may find that step difficult and could benefit from seeing the topic more as a skill.

Activities on the theme of calculation are a good way to clarify the key ESP teaching principle of what has been called the 'non-trivial' comprehension question. (Wilson, J 1986) Here, comprehension is not demonstrated by a student presenting a paraphrase of a part of a text, but by having to solve a problem in the manner written about or by performing some other text-related task. Obviously, mathematical explanations lend themselves to this kind of task-based process. However, some of these questions can make ESP teachers feel insecure by taking them too far into an unfamiliar specialisation, others can be answered by students using old knowledge. A compromise is an activity such as 'new numerals', where students are involved in tasks that are both accessible to the teacher and sufficiently unusual for the students to demonstrate understanding of the test.

The chapter begins with an activity to help students manipulate larger numbers in English. 5.2 is about ordinals. 5.3 further explores the language of calculation. In 5.4, the issue is wording problems. 5.5 looks at ratios and percentages through the theme of map-making. 5.6 and 5.7 are about measuring wealth. In 5.8 the concern is algebra, while 5.9 touches on what algebraic symbols mean. 5.10 and 5.11 use questionnaires to get students talking about ratios, percentages, averages and probabilities. 5.12 raises the question of why numbers are written in the way that they are.

5.1

FOCUS
Using larger
numbers

LEVEL
Elementary to
intermediate

TIME
20–30 minutes

NUMBER BREAKDOWN

Even native speakers can have difficulty reading off larger numbers. The insertion of commas makes the task easier (e.g. 7,123). A way to help foreign learners is to insert even clearer breaks in the number.

Procedure

1 Check that students know the following:

$$100 = \text{a hundred}$$
$$1,000 = \text{a thousand}$$
$$1,000,000 = \text{a million}$$

2 Write this table on the board. You can have as many rows as you like.

million(s)	thousand(s)	hundred(s)	ten(s) (-ty(s))	one(s)

3 Write this number on the board: 378
4 Get a student to say it. As they do so fill in the table as follows:

million(s)	thousand(s)	hundred(s)	ten(s) (-ty(s))	one(s)
		3	7	8

5 Rub out the number. Say another four-figure number and get a student to fill in the table accordingly.
6 Ask another student to say the number in the table. If they have trouble, point to the figure under 'thousand(s)', get them to say it, point to 'thousand(s)' so that they read that, then repeat with the other boxes as necessary.
7 Repeat with five-, six-, seven- and eight-figure numbers.
8 Ask students to copy the table onto a sheet of paper without any numbers in the boxes. The table should cover the whole sheet.
9 Dictate a series of large numbers then get students to transcribe them into the table.
10 Put students into pairs A and B. The A's dictate the numbers they have just written down in their table to the Bs who write them down as numerals on a scrap of paper. The Bs then read these numerals back to the As who help them by checking what they put in their table.

EXTENSION

11 Companies dealing with large sums of money often use cheques which are laid out like the table above. Draw a blank cheque on the board, substituting the table for where you would normally

write how much you are paying in words. Ask students to copy it. Set up a small role play (e.g. accountant to word processor operator) where you are dictating a series of sums to be made payable to different people.

12 Under their cheques, students write a table with several boxes in each column (e.g. six). You take the role of the accountant while students enter the sums into the tables.

13 Put the students into pairs. They take it in turns to be the accountant and the word processor operator.

IN ORDER OF WHAT?

5.2

FOCUS
Ordinals,
'according to'
phrases

LEVEL
Elementary to
intermediate

TIME
30 minutes

Ordinals are not just important in themselves but because they are the basis of fractions of less than a quarter and of all related expressions. They also crop up in activities related to ranking or comparing.

In Class

1 Make sure that students know their ordinal numbers.
2 Read students the following list of continents:

First, Asia
Second, North America
Third, South America
Fourth, Australia
Fifth, Antarctica
Sixth, Europe

3 Ask students to suggest why you have ranked the continents in this order. Is it according to size, economic power, population, living standards, cultural interest or what? They should discuss the ranking and agree or disagree.

4 Ask students to compile lists: lists of countries, cities in one country, great cities of the world, oceans, companies, planets, atomic systems, materials, paintings; anything that takes their fancy.

5 Ask students to rank the items in each list according to some criterion, obvious or not so obvious. (I once had a student who ranked cities according to the worth of their opera houses, another ranked elements according to the number of electrons in their atomic system.)

6 Students read out their lists. Others discuss the ranking and decide the criterion. If they have difficulty, ask the student who read out the list to give clues. Set a time limit of about three minutes per list. After the answer has been given, the class can contest the order.

EXTENSION

If your students get on well, then they can rank each other according to hidden criteria. They then get into pairs and try to guess each other's criteria. The pairs keep the guesses to themselves.

5.3

FOCUS
The language of calculation, asking for things

LEVEL
Beginner to upper intermediate

TIME
20 minutes

EXTRAS
Five or six cards for each student; one calculator for every two students (optional)

GETTING YOUR NUMBER

This is a lively number collection activity. It can be orientated towards students' needs by the kind of numbers you choose and the way you write them.

BEFORE CLASS
Write a number on a card for each student.

In Class

1 Give each student a card with a simple number and four or five blank or cards for trading. Ask each to rewrite their number on each trading card in a different way.

e.g. At a basic level:
The simple number 4 could give four different cards each with one of the following:
$104 - 100$ $4/2 \times 2$ 8×0.5 $(7 + 3) - 6$

At a higher level:
1154 could give: $1000 + 200 - 46$ $2(1125 + 7) - 1103$
$(28/2 \times 11) + 1000$ $11\,000 \times 0.1 - 18 + 72$

2 Redistribute all the cards so that each student has a simple number they did not have before and four or five trading cards which express different numbers.

3 Ask each student to collect a family of trading cards that express their simple number only. They do this by reading out a trading card they don't want in turns. The rest listen to the expression, write it down and work it out. If they hear one that is the equivalent of their simple number they swap another for it. Continue until all students have all their cards.

STORY TELLING BY NUMBERS

5.4

FOCUS
Understanding
problems, text
development,
interactive
information
transfer, writing
about the past

LEVEL
Elementary to
intermediate

TIME
40 minutes

Here, students have to get numerical information out of a text and understand simple arithmetical problems.

BEFORE CLASS

Think back to the kind of arithmetical story problems you used to do in school. Use the example below or write or find two such problems. Adapt the problems to the kind of students you have and to whatever kinds of numbers you are studying (percentages, currencies, decimals etc.). I wrote the following example:

My father bought three hectares of land from his uncle. My grandfather gave us another hectare. In 1970 the value of the land was £20,000. The value of the land increased by 15 per cent a year for ten years. My father sold a hectare in 1980 to pay for my grandfather's funeral. The funeral cost £8,000. How much was left to put in the bank?

In Class

1 Tell the class that you are going to read them a problem. They should concentrate only on the numbers and note these down so that they can make the necessary calculations.

2 Read the problem at normal speed. Repeat as many times as necessary for the better students to determine the figures and calculate the answer. Advise students that even if they can calculate in their heads they should write down each stage clearly and neatly as if in an elementary maths class.

3 Ask for the correct answer. When somebody gives it to you, ask them to come to the board and to write up their calculations step by step.

4 Ask another student to recount the story. They should use the numbers as prompts.

5 Get the students to write a different story to fit the calculations on the board.

6 Ask students to read their stories to the class.

EXTENSION

7 Get students to write their own problems.

8 Form pairs. Student A reads their problem to student B who writes down the information needed to solve it. Students A and B swap roles.

9 One student comes to the board and writes up the calculations for their partner's problem. The rest of the class have five minutes to try to improvise stories around the numbers then they tell their stories in turn.

5.5

FOCUS
Mapping a place,
talking about
measurements
and ratios

LEVEL
Elementary to
advanced

TIME
40 minutes

EXTRAS
A set of rulers

THE MAP-MAKER

Diagram dictation is an old ESP standby and can be applied to many subject areas. This version is interesting because it forces students to pay close attention to their immediate environment and engages them in calculating and measuring.

In Class

1 Check that students can express ratios/scales (e.g. 1 inch to the mile) also measurements: (e.g. 30 metres wide, 300 kilometres long, 30 metres from A to B, 7 metres high etc.), and directions: (e.g. north, east, south-west, NE or NNE).

2 Ask students to close their eyes and to think about their house and where it is situated. Tell them to remember next-door buildings, nearby landmarks and streets along with their dimensions and the distances between them.

3 Tell students to imagine then draw a map showing an area of one square kilometre around their house (one square mile if your students need to learn imperial measurements). They should decide on a scale, bearing in mind the size of their paper. They should include important landmarks such as train stations and large buildings. They should try to keep everything to scale, indicate distances and also show topography (hills, valleys, slopes etc.).

4 Form pairs A/B back to back. Ask the A's to dictate their map to the Bs. They should be as exact as possible and give all measurements as they are in reality and not to scale (e.g. if a train station is 0.5 km from their house they say 'half a kilometre' not 'one centimetre'). A tells which corner B is starting in then works up and across. Student A should not say where their house is. They must remember that time is limited. The A's should try to help the Bs but must not see the map while it is being drawn.

5 The A's show their map to the Bs. The Bs must then try to mark where their house is.

EXTENSION
6 Bs and As swap roles.

TRUE EXPRESSIONS, FALSE IMPRESSIONS

This is another activity that both tackles numeracy and the language of numeracy. It adapts well to your class's level of numeracy and of language.

BEFORE CLASS

Find out from the students what areas of mathematics they have covered. Locate textbooks in those areas and copy down key equations. Write down a series of arithmetical expressions that include the types of number to be practised. Half should be true and half false.

e.g. $2 > 3$ $6 + 3 = 9$ $75 < 18$ $28 + 10 > 60$
$458 = 300 + 122 + 36$ $95/7 = 19*5/9-2$
$11051 - 40 + 11 > 120000/10 - 949$

In Class

1 Check that the students know how to read out the symbols you want to work with. Show students a few dozen symbols and ask them which they understand. Work only with these. Use the appendix after this activity for symbols and their readings.
2 Ask students to write true and false equations and give them to you for reading out.
3 Form pairs A/B. Tell the A's that they are 'false' and the Bs that they are 'true'.
4 Tell the students that you are going to read some expressions to them slowly, some true, some false. The A's write down the true expressions and the Bs the false.
5 Read the expressions slowly, repeat if asked.
6 A's form pairs with Bs. The pairs compare lists so that each student can produce one complete list of true and false expressions.

Appendix

Symbol	Reading
$+$	plus
$-$	minus
$\times$	times
$\div$	divided by
$>$	more than
$<$	less than
$\geq$	greater than or equal
$\leq$	less than or equal
$\neq$	not equal to

5.6

FOCUS
The language of calculation, expressing difference and equality

LEVEL
Beginner to upper intermediate

TIME
25 minutes

Symbol	Reading
$\int_a^b$	integral from a to b
$\sqrt{}$	square root
$\sqrt[n]{}$	nth root
x^n	x to nth power
f'	f prime
$\dfrac{df}{dx}$	dfdx
$\dfrac{df}{dx}\mid a$	derivative of
$f'(a)$	f at a
α	alpha
β	beta
γ	gamma
δ	delta
ϵ	epsilon
$\dfrac{\partial f}{\partial x}$	partial of f with respect to x
x_n	x sub n
$\approx$	approximately
x_0	x nought
EX	expectations of X
VarX	variance of X
cov (x,y)	covariance of X and Y
i.o.	infinitely often
w.p.1	with probability one
$\xrightarrow{p}$	convergence in probability
$\rightarrow$	converges
$\lim\limits_{n\to\infty} a_n = a$	lim of a subn equals a as n converges to infinity
$\lim\limits_{x\to c} f(x) = b$	limit of f of x as x converges to c equals b
lXY	correlation coefficient between X and Y
$a_n \to a \to$ as $n \to \infty$	a subn converges to infinity as n goes to infinity

NOT MUCH FOR A LIFE

Here, students measure wealth not distance. They use the language of profit and loss but in an affective frame.

In Class

1 Write the following on the left side of the board. Ask students to suggest figures for each item as you go. Explain that the £000 indicates that you are working in thousands of pounds, so you write one million as £1000. (This is standard practice in Accountancy.)

Profit and Loss Account
Sales
Cost of sales
Gross profit
Management expenses
Selling and distribution expenses
Directors' fees and salaries
Interest on overdrafts and loans
Net trading profit
Corporation tax
Profit for the year retained

Take care that figures are consistent.

e.g. *Cost of sales* should not exceed *sales* (unless the company is heading for bankruptcy).
Gross profit is obtained by deducting *the cost of sales* from *sales*.
Net trading profit is *expenses, salaries* and *loans* deducted from *gross profit*.
Corporation tax is a percentage of the *net trading profit*. Students should decide what this percentage is then calculate accordingly.
Profit for the year retained is *net profit* less *corporation tax*.

2 Write the following phrases on the right side of the board in a column in random order beside the account:
● what I have achieved
● what my achievements have cost me in time and energy
● the value to me of my year
● time spent in essential but boring tasks to make the achievement possible
● time spent reaching and persuading people
● the cost of getting others to help me run my life
● what I owe to others
● what I have left after my dues to others are paid
● what I owe to society in general
● what is really my own

5.7

FOCUS
Profit and loss, talking about how one has spent one's time

LEVEL
Lower intermediate to advanced

TIME
30–40 minutes

3 Tell students to imagine that the profit and loss account expresses the worth of their year to themselves and its cost. Get them to try to attach a meaning to each item.

e.g.   sales = what I have achieved
         cost of sales = what my achievements have cost me in time and energy

The phrases on the right of the board are a guide to how they could interpret the items in the account column.

4 Students work individually at preparing an account assessing the worth of their past year to them. If they cost some items negatively and others at nothing, then that is their affair.

5 In pairs or small groups, students discuss their accounts with each other, explaining their entries and costings.

RATIONALE

The activity arises out of the affective principle which holds that a lesson is made more memorable by being applied to the student's own life. Many other types of specialised language can be made more interesting by being made into a metaphor with which the student describes their own predicament.

MARKET-MAKER

This is a very good way to get students reading and talking about currency movements and stock market indices. It requires a little forethought because you will have to keep a couple or more back copies of a financial paper, but once this is done, the activity is easy to set up and run and can provide a useful discussion topic or filler throughout a business English course.

In Class

1 Check that students understand these types of investment: stocks, shares, gilts, currencies, unit trusts, investment trusts.

If there are problems, you can explain as follows: A **share** is any of the equal parts into which the ownership of a company can be divided, which are offered for sale to the public. A **dividend** is that part of the money made by a business, which is divided among those who own shares in the business (usu. twice a year). (*) A shareholder (or stockholder in AmE) is the owner of shares in a business.

An **investment (trust) company** is a limited company (LDBE) that uses its capital to buy securities as investment, hoping to make a profit from dividends and interest received and from capital gains on sales of securities. Such companies are often called investment trusts, although they are seldom real trusts. (**)

In Britain, a **unit trust**, is an organisation that collects money from subscribers, called unit holders, usu. small investors, and invests it in securities for their benefit . . . Unlike an investment trust a unit trust is not a company and units are not traded on the Stock Exchange. (**)

Currency is the particular type of money in use in a country. (*)

Gilts or **gilt edged securities** are fixed-interest securities issued or guaranteed by the British Government. They are securities of the highest class, considered by investors to be without any financial risk.

2 Divide the class into two groups, A and B. Give each group a back-copy of your paper and a calculator.

5.8

FOCUS
Currencies, ratios, negotiating

LEVEL
Intermediate to advanced

TIME
40 minutes (This activity is suitable to use as a regular feature across a course, following financial trends on a daily or weekly basis)

EXTRAS
Two or more back copies of the same edition of the *Financial Times* or of the financial pages of another broadsheet paper. It should be between a week and a month old. Two or more up-to-date copies of the same paper. Two or more calculators (optional)

* Longman Dictionary of English Language and Culture
** Longman Dictionary of Business English

3 Draw four columns on the board with headings in the way shown:

Holding	Number of units	Unit price	Total value

Then write 'Value of the portfolio on:' with the day's date, at the bottom of the board.

Explain that these columns show the value and make-up of an investment portfolio. The 'holding' shows what you have invested in (e.g. Swiss francs, gilts, China Trust, BP shares). The number of units is how many shares, francs or bonds you have bought. The unit price is how much each share, gilt or franc cost in sterling. The total value is the total cost of the holding or the number of units multiplied by the unit price.

4 Tell each group that they are a consortium with one billion pounds to invest. They have fifteen minutes to decide how to invest the money. They must invest for capital growth and can choose the currency markets, the stock markets, unit trusts, treasury bonds (gilts) or any investment medium that is listed in their paper. They cannot invest more than a tenth of their wealth in any one holding, but apart from this, they can balance their portfolio in any way they choose. They must remember that income will not be included in any calculation about the portfolio's increase or growth. Advise them to split the newspaper up among their group so that different students can read about different investment opportunities. They can also bring their own knowledge of recent market trends to bear. When the fifteen minutes are up they must present you with a complete portfolio set out on a piece of paper in the way shown on the board.

5 Give students five minutes' warning to start getting their portfolio finalised and written down, then call time.

6 Tell the groups to swap portfolios. Hand out your up-to-date copies of the paper and get each group to revalue the other's portfolio according to that paper. They can ask for help to find a particular share or currency listing.

7 Bring a student to the board. Ask group A to dictate their valuation of B's portfolio while the student writes it on the board then vice versa. Allow for discussion and corrections. The group with the highest valuation wins.

EXTENSION

8 Take in copies of the valuation.

9 After about a week, hand out the copies and get group A students to do another valuation of B's portfolio and vice versa for homework. The next day, get one A and one B student to report back to the class on the value of the other group's portfolio. Repeat two or three times.

10 Ask students to draw a line graph showing the performance of the portfolio. Select one student from each group to describe their graphs and explain progress to date.

RATIONALE

Scanning a document then homing in on essential parts of it is an important ESP/EAP skill. Students here have to do just that to find out how to build a portfolio. They then have to discuss and calculate values, putting the relevant language into play. The extension provides useful practice in describing trends. When used regularly, this activity can generate real interest in financial trends.

GROUP EXPRESSIONS

5.9

This is a straightforward exercise for using the language of algebra. It is based on established whole-class story-telling techniques.

FOCUS
Mathematical expressions

BEFORE CLASS

Make one set of the following cards, two sets for a class of more than fourteen, three for more than twenty-eight, etc.

LEVEL
Elementary to intermediate

TIME
15 minutes

squared	=
cubed	square root of
to the power of	<
of	>
–	open/close brackets
+	number
=	letter

In Class

1 If your class has more than fourteen students, divide it into groups of between seven and ten. If you have cards prepared, distribute them round each group. If you have no cards, get each student in a group to write down at least one of the above words or phrases on a piece of paper.
2 Appoint a student as secretary in each group.
3 Tell the students that they are going to construct a mathematical expression. The first student says what is on their card, then puts it face down in front of them. If they have a phrase or word that can only follow something else (e.g. *to the power of*) then they say 'pass'. They must do everything they can to keep the expression meaningful. Students with 'letter' or 'number' cards can add in any appropriate number. Students keep their cards until the expression is thought to be finished. Each student may have several turns, adding in letters or numbers before one expression is finished. The secretary must write each expression down as it is built up. When as many cards have been played as possible, the secretary reads back the expression to the class who decide if it is meaningful.
4 Start the activity with one group to show how it works. If a student hesitates for more than a few seconds go on to the next, then come back to them. When the class have got the idea, start them off in their separate groups.
5 Redistribute the cards within each group and repeat.

5.10

FOCUS
Describing formulae, changes of state, statements of equality

LEVEL
Elementary to advanced

TIME
30–40 minutes

POETIC EXPRESSION

This shows how to use some of the language of algebra then to reapply it to a more general and unusual context. The activity may seem strange to some, since it asks students to venture outside their normal ESP mode. However, students often feel overloaded with too much technical input and this type of activity is a way to give them some variety while still giving them relevant language.

In Class

1 Check that students can dictate equations in English. (See 5.6 for symbols and glosses.)
2 Remind the students that the letters in an algebraic expression represent something else, numbers for example.
3 Ask students to invent and write down any expression they like as long as it is not too complicated. e.g. $X - Y = Z$
4 Ask students to dictate their expression to a neighbour who redictates it to a neighbour on the other side, and so on.
5 Stop the exercise after each student has written down about five expressions.

6 Ask students to look carefully at the last expression they wrote down. Tell them it is a statement about their life. Each symbol represents something important to them. They must decide what the symbols represent. You could give them this as an example:

X = my life
Y = a wife
Z = a desert

However, they cannot just declare the symbols to represent anything they like. They must make their expression meaningful. Here is an example from a Saudi student:

$$x \quad - \quad y \quad = \quad z^2$$
my life minus a wife becomes a desert squared

Students can change their expressions in order to make sense out of them.

7 When the class have finished giving meaning to their expressions, bring one of your better students to the board.

8 Different students dictate their expression not as symbols but as words. The student at the board rewrites the words as an algebraic expression. Invite the rest of the class to help.

e.g.   Student A: *My life minus a wife becomes a desert squared.*
Student B (writes): $a - b = c^2$

Repeat with a few students.

EXTENSION

9 Tell everyone that you would like their statements to sound less mathematical and more poetic. Suggest that they change their statements as little as possible, but enough to make them read like tiny poems. Offer the following example:

Before:
My life minus a wife becomes a desert squared.
After:
My life without a wife
turns to a great desert.

10 Students exchange poems then read out each others' to the class.

5.11

FOCUS
Ratios,
percentages,
question and
answer practice,
report-writing

LEVEL
Lower
intermediate to
advanced; see the
variation for
elementary

TIME
50–60 minutes

FIELD SURVEY

This questionnaire-based activity provides an opportunity to practise applying the language of ratios, percentages and averages. Reflecting scientific method, it moves from prediction to experiment.

BEFORE CLASS
Think up a list of topics along the following lines:
love-life/family relationships, preferred kinds of possessions (house ownership etc.), job satisfaction/interest, artistic/literary/musical tastes, general leisure interests, eating habits, ways of getting about/transportation, preferred holidays/time off, political views/social/religious attitudes, social class, educational attitudes, choice of career.

In Class

1 Form pairs. Allocate a different topic to each pair.
2 Ask students to think carefully about what their topic involves. Extend their ideas if necessary, e.g. for 'class': *What does it mean to be middle or working class? Is it how much money you have or something more?*
3 Say that each pair will construct a 5–10 item questionnaire to determine class attitudes in their topic areas. The questions should be multiple choice or have yes/no answers, e.g.

Do you think of yourself as: upper class?
                                  middle class?
                                  working class?

To determine class, money is: unimportant?
                                  important?
                                  very important?

Each student keeps a copy of their questionnaire.
4 Students predict how their questions will be answered in straight ratios or percentages e.g. *90% will think they are middle class.*
5 Get students to circulate in order to find different people to answer their questionnaires. Allow 15–20 minutes for this stage. Do not expect everybody to interview everyone else unless the class is very small.
6 Bring the pairs back together when students appear to have interviewed a reasonable sample. Ask students to calculate the result as ratios and as percentages. They should average the results from both partner's questionnaires to do this.
7 Each pair tells the class the main thing that their questionnaire was trying to find out. The other students try to predict the result. The pair say if any of the predictions were correct.

EXTENSION

8 Either:

Get students to write reports presenting their findings using the format given in activity 2.1 School Reports.

Or:

Give students 15 minutes to circulate freely and find out everything they can about each others' questionnaire results. They should then write a general survey of class opinion using experiment report format.

VARIATIONS

a At step 4, students complete their questionnaires with classmates or students from other classes for homework.

b For elementary students: at step 2, simplify the task and reduce the number of questions.

> e.g. **Topic:** Love-life
> **To find out:** How many people are happily married.
> **Questions:** Are you married?
> Are you happy?
> Do you have a girl/boyfriend? etc.

NEW NUMBERS

5.12

In this activity, students express their understanding of a text by inventing and manipulating new types of number. The exercise helps students to understand how numbers are built and how the way we write them down influences the way we calculate.

In Class

1 Hand out the text and ask students to read it to themselves.
2 As they are finishing, write the following on the board:

> The text tells you about a different number system. For this system you will need two additional numerals for 10 and 11. Invent those numerals. Write them in any way you like.

3 Ask the class to write ten numbers greater than twenty using their new system. If they are adept, get them to make the numbers run from two digits up to five or more.

> e.g. | arabic system | new system |
> |---|---|
> | 144 | 100 |
> | 1584 | *00 (*=11) |
> | 20760 | 10024 |

4 Form pairs. Ask them to swap their new numbers, then to try reading them to each other (this may take some time).

FOCUS
Reading comprehension, calculating, thinking about numbers

LEVEL
Lower intermediate

TIME
30 minutes

EXTRAS
A class set of a text (below)

5 Ask students to divide their numbers by 144. Get them to say these quotients back to each other. If some students don't understand that this operation is simply a case of moving a decimal point two places to the left, bring one to the board to explain (12 is written as 10, therefore $100 = 12 \times 12 = 144$ in normal numbers). Next, ask students to divide their numbers by six as fast as possible. Get them to call out their answers.

EXTENSION

6 Ask the class if they found it difficult to work with strange numerals. Ask them if they see any relationship between this difficulty and that of learning a new language.

Text for Activity 5.12

Ten is the first number that combines two digits. We only have ten simple digits in the Arabic system: 0 1 2 3 4 5 6 7 8 9. If you want to find out what a huge advance this system was, then try doing long division with Roman numbers! The Romans had the same problem. They could not use their numbers to calculate and had to devise other systems. However, the Arabic system is not perfect. A better system might have been based on multiples of twelve not ten. In this system '10' means twelve. This might have been better because twelve is a much easier number to manipulate. Twelve can be divided by 2,3,4 and 6 whereas ten can only be divided by 2 and 5.

CHAPTER 6

Data-mapping

Interpreting graphs and diagrams is important in many occupations and academic disciplines. Some ESP teachers encounter students who need practice in the skill of interpretation itself. Others deal with learners for whom this is second nature, but who perhaps lack the language in which to express what they know. Some students need the listening and reading skills that are an essential prerequisite of the ability to extract the data they wish to express diagrammatically. The following activities are then likely to be useful to students from very varied specialisations. They are also likely to be interesting to teachers who are looking for non-verbal ways of eliciting language or testing understanding that have more relevance to life than the picture-based practice of the traditional EFL classroom.

In this chapter, activities 6.1–6.4 deal with graphs. The language of comparing is practised through bar graphs, then that of trends through line graphs. 6.4 looks at the relationship of different kinds of text to different types of graph. The activity 6.5 shifts the focus to the naming of shapes and the description of plans. 6.6 looks at how to build up a systems description from diagrams of its parts. 6.7 uses a diagram as the prompt for a traditional structure exercise that is in turn made into the basis of a more authentic kind of discourse. 6.8 explores the potential of organisation charts.

LAND BARS

This exercise gets students to express their reactions to landscape as a bar graph.

In Class

1 Ask the class to imagine that they are in a landscape that they know well and is important to them. This could be their home, a place they would like to make their home or somewhere they lived in the past. They should ask themselves how the place touches them emotionally and why, what meaning its features may have, whether they would like to exploit this landscape and for what.

2 Write *topography* on the board. One student describes the place they have been thinking about, dealing only with what it looks like.

3 Write *affective* on the board. The same student describes how the landscape touched or affected them.

4 Write *symbolism* on the board. Ask if features or things in that student's landscape represent or symbolise something generally or to particular individuals. A church spire, for example, is built in order to symbolise something to all people, a particular tree might signify 'childhood' to one person because they climbed it when they were small.

5 Ask if there is something in the scene that they think of as usable in some way. This could be a forest that will keep their fire burning or a street that gets them where they want quickly. Write *functionality* on the board.

6 Sketch the bar graph (fig. 4) on the board. Explain that the graph shows a person's responses to landscape. Ask them how they think this particular person responded to a landscape.

    e.g. For fig. 4: the person was not very moved by a place (affectivity) and did not see its features as having many meanings for them. However, they remembered what the landscape looked like in considerable detail (topography).

7 Form pairs. Exclude the student you have already interviewed. The A students interview the Bs about their landscapes, asking them to describe what their landscape looks like (topography), how it affects them (affectivity), what it means to them (symbolism) and how they could use it (functionality). They should pay close attention to how much their partner talks about each topic and also how forced their interest in it is. Explain how some people may describe what it looks like in detail and others may talk more as if it were full of hidden meaning. The Bs and As swap roles. The excluded student interviews you then helps you monitor the pairwork.

6.1

FOCUS
Describing and sketching bar graphs, discussing responses to landscape, comparing

LEVEL
Lower intermediate to advanced

TIME
40–50 minutes

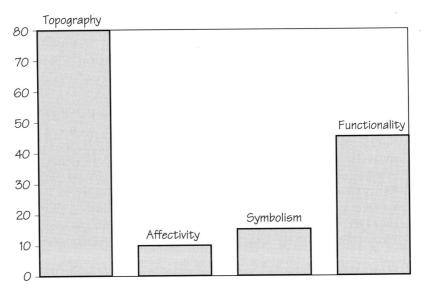

Fig. 4

8 Working alone, each student draws up a similar graph showing the relative strengths of their partner's responses to landscape. For example, if their partner talked a lot about what the place looked like but said 'places don't move me, it's my home and that's it,' they could score high on topography and low on affectivity, as in fig. 4. However, they should also try to think about the strength and nature of the response and remember that the topics do not always separate out. Thus a topographical description can sound functional (e.g. 'an area of good farm land shielded by trees) or affective (beautiful red soil surrounded by old trees). Also, an excited tone and a use of affective adjectives (beautiful, delightful etc.) might indicate a high affective score even if a lot of time has been spent on description. Make clear that you are looking for a rough, subjective measure.

9 When students have drawn their graph, they should show it to the partner and discuss how far it represents their partner's true response to landscape.

EXTENSION

10 Working alone, each student writes a short paragraph describing the graphs as if in the results statement of an experiment report. They should give their imprecise, subjective measure an objective authority, e.g.

The subject's response to topography was strong at 70. By contrast, the affectivity response was low at 30 and symbolism too weak to measure. etc.

You can use this as an example of how the report genre can give an objective authority to something it does not really have.

TALKING TRENDS

An ability to discuss trends is not just essential to science and commerce, it is also part of the conversational armoury of anybody interested in the wider world, current affairs, cultural issues, history or politics.

In Class

1 On the board sketch a line graph as in fig. 5, but without the labels, while students copy.

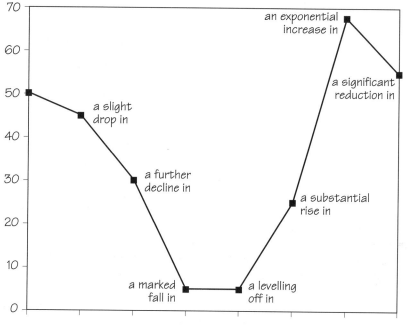

Fig. 5

6.2

FOCUS
Interpreting line graphs, talking about trends

LEVEL
Lower intermediate to advanced

TIME
40 minutes

2 Write the following phrases on the board:

an increase in   a levelling off in   a decline in   a fall in
a drop in   a rise in   a reduction in

And write these adjectives underneath:

noticeable   marked   substantial   slight   perceptible
large   small   exponential

Answer questions about meaning and pronunciation.

3 Get students to say phrases combining the adjectives and the noun phrases:

e.g. *a marked increase in*

This should be a rapid practice to help students get their tongues round the phrases.

4 Select a topic: e.g. 'rainfall', 'the rate of inflation' or 'traffic accidents'. Read out a complete phrase:

e.g. *a marked increase in traffic accidents*

And get students to label a part of the graph that illustrates 'a marked increase'. Repeat using all the phrases in random order. Check that students have labelled the graph correctly. They should now understand fig. 5.

5 Choose a trend, for example: *illegitimate births in Upper Syldavia.* Do a class graph dictation illustrating the trend. The teacher begins and says something like: *In 1960 there was a marked increase in illegitimate births in Upper Syldavia.* The rest of the class start to draw the graph. A student continues with another phrase: *In 1961 there was a slight levelling off.*
Go on round the class until all the phrases have been used up. Students should not label the graphs at this stage.

6 Form pairs and ask each to label and to compare their graphs.

6.3

FOCUS
Graphs

LEVEL
Elementary to upper intermediate

TIME
20 minutes

TRENDS AGAIN

Here the student's life is the trend to be discussed.

In Class

1 Ask the class to close their eyes, relax and imagine their life as one long graph with all its ups and down. Ask them to picture their graph mentally.

2 After a few minutes, get students to draw the graph of their life, year by year. Adult students may need to concentrate on their adult life.

3 Form pairs A and B. The As and Bs exchange graphs. The As try to interpret the Bs' graphs and the As put them right as necessary.

VARIATION
EOP students map their careers, projecting them into the future.

ONE OF THREE

This activity gets students thinking about the right way to map data and about how that map can in turn effect the way they describe something.

In Class

1 Sketch one example of a line, bar and pie graph on the board. Form groups of four or five and ask the groups to suggest something that each graph is trying to show. Tell the students that this is not a guessing game. Any plausible answer will be treated as correct. Also, each graph can be treated as dealing with a completely separate idea.

2 A student from each group comes up and explains the graph as if it were part of a presentation. The rest of the class takes notes.

3 After the presentations, ask students to look at their notes and ask if they think that a particular kind of information fits a particular kind of graph. For example, are bar graphs better for comparing different measurements? Try to say as little as possible at this point. Ask students whether they think one graph tended to elicit a particular type of language more than another. For example: did they hear more talk of percentages in relation to pie graphs? Do line graphs need a more dynamic kind of language with more verbs suggesting movement?

4 Tell the class that you are going to read them three short texts. They must decide whether to represent each text as a line, bar or pie graph.

5 Read the texts once. Give the students a minute to make up their minds on how they would draw each one. Tell them they will hear them again, but that this time they must make notes, paying particular attention to facts and figures so that they can draw the graphs.

6 Read slowly and repeat passages when asked. Ask each student to produce a different type of graph for each passage.

7 Bring three students to the board. One sketches their pie graph, the other their line graph and the other their bar. Ask the class to decide which graph refers to which text. If there is disagreement and students have not mapped each text in the same way then explain that:

passage one fits a bar graph well because it shows differences between set quantities; passage two shows a fluctuating trend and needs a line graph to plot movement between points; passage three describes the parts of a whole and is therefore best illustrated by a pie chart.

8 Distribute the texts and ask students if what they said about language and graphs is born out by what they find in the texts.

6.4

FOCUS
Comparing statistics, describing trends, sketching pie, bar and line graphs

LEVEL
Lower to upper intermediate

TIME
30 minutes

EXTRAS
A class set of three texts in a suitable area of study along the following lines – one can be represented as a line graph, one as a bar graph and one as a pie chart. Leave out the words that say the kind of graph it describes. (See the example texts below)

Example Texts for Activity 6.4

Text 1 (line graph)

The link between prices and political stability becomes clearer when one looks at the average annual price of wheat on the Paris market between 1650 and 1660. The decade began with the relatively high price of 25 units. The deterioration in the political situation drove the price up to 30 units the year after. The price was lower at 25 in 1653 and fell to 20 the year after that. It was lower still in 1655 at 17, then at 15 in 1656. The price was then stable until 1658 when it rose slightly to 16 units. It was 20 by the decade's end.

(From Braudel, F 1978, p. 59)

Text 2 (bar graph)

Also interesting is the way the prices fluctuate wildly at times of crisis. During 1650 they fell from 30 to almost 20, rose to 25 then fell again to 20 before rising towards 25 at the year's end. The rise continued towards 30 in the first part of the critical 1652, then was held with some minor fluctuations in the bands 25 to 30. The price shoots up to 35 during the last part of the year and declines precipitously at the beginning of 1653, finishing near 15 at the end of the year.

(From Braudel, F 1979, p. 58)

Text 3 (pie chart)

As late as 1780, 45% of the Danish population are estimated to have been involved in agriculture as against 10% in manufacturing. 5% were engaged in commerce and another 5% in fishing and sailing. 25% were engaged in some form of unskilled labour and a further 10% had no identifiable occupation.

(From Braudel, F 1979, p. 253)

BUILDING DESIGN

Here, students talk about building plans by describing the shapes that the plans incorporate. The activity uses the technique of diagram dictation from memory.

In Class

1 Draw the shapes in fig. 6 on the board and mislabel all of them. As you draw, your class may become agitated by the crassness of your errors. Do not say anything until all the shapes have been mislabelled. Then say simply: OK? as if about to carry on. When they protest and put you right, say something like: *Oh I see, so that's a rectangle*, as if you were very ignorant. Then keep on asking: *Is that OK now?* until everything has been correctly labelled.

6.5

FOCUS
Talking about shapes, describing plans

LEVEL
Elementary to upper-intermediate

TIME
30 minutes

EXTRAS
One copy of a building plan that incorporates most of the shapes below (See fig. 7)

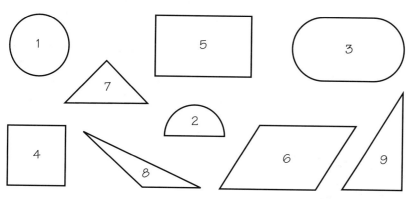

Fig. 6

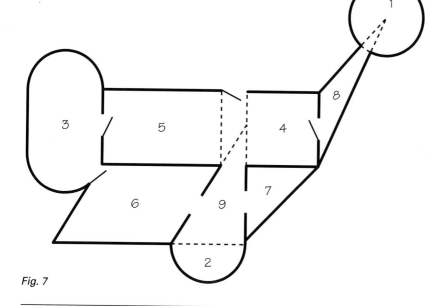

Fig. 7

2 Tell the class that they are going to draw the floor plan of a building. This building must incorporate all the shapes on the board in some way and look as normal as possible. Explain that one needn't draw a room based on every shape. Their plans can look more realistic if some rooms combine two, or even three, shapes.

3 To demonstrate the activity, ask a student to dictate their plan to you. Draw it on the board as they speak. Take in their plan and give them the one that you have prepared (fig. 7). Ask them to work with this during step 5.

4 Give students a minute or two to memorise their plans, then take them in.

5 Form pairs A and B. Set up a role play where A is a client and B is an architect. The As describe their plan to the Bs as if discussing the house they want to build. B makes suggestions and draws the plan.

RATIONALE

There are two areas of language practice here: describing plans and naming shapes. This language is often practised with straight diagram dictation. Diagram dictation produces an odd tension where the student who takes down the plan that their partner is dictating is unsure whether they should be helping or hindering the process. Here, the task is cooperative and the language elicited richer for that.

6.6

FOCUS
Linking components into a system

LEVEL
Beginner to upper intermediate

TIME
20–30 minutes

SYSTEMS SOLUTIONS

Here students use diagrams to build up a system.

BEFORE CLASS

1 Select a system that can be represented diagrammatically. The parts of the system must be easy to represent on their own. Fig. 8 shows the components of simple electrical systems.

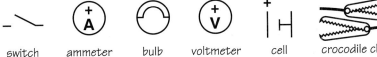

switch   ammeter   bulb   voltmeter   cell   crocodile clips

Fig. 8

In Class

1 Draw the parts of the system on the board and ask students to identify them.
2 Give the class a minute or two to ask how they could connect all the components into a system.
3 Divide the board into four sections. Bring a student (A) to the board to draw in the first section while somebody in the class (B) dictates their way of connecting the parts.
4 Ask up to three students with alternative systems to dictate them while (A) draws in each of the other sections.
5 Ask what the systems shown might be used for. Rub out those which do not have an obvious function and which do not make sense. Ask for alternatives if the class has any.

EXTENSION
6 Ask students to write explanations of the diagrams left on the board.

VARIATION
At step 5, sketch a map on the board, showing towns, villages, rivers etc. but no infrastructure (roads, paths, railways, power-lines, gas and water mains). Ask students to list necessities and then design an effective infrastructure. They should remember that the further you have to bring water, gas or electricity the more it costs, while a major source such as a reservoir needs a certain population density to be economic. There are also pollution considerations. Thus, it may be economic to put power stations in or near cities, but the people will not welcome this. Students should also avoid choke points in their traffic system and generally plan an infrastructure that fosters economic development, and avoids natural obstacles.

ONE THING LEADS TO ANOTHER

In this activity, a diagram prompts a traditional structure exercise. This formal type of language practice is then turned into one that is more natural and less disjointed.

BEFORE CLASS
Decide on a cause and effect chain that is relevant to your class, e.g.

When a solid is heated, energy is transferred to its molecules. When energy is transferred to the molecules, they vibrate more but stay in their fixed position. When the molecules vibrate, they need more space. When the molecules need more space, the solid expands. When still more energy is added, the molecules begin to move past each other. When the molecules begin to move past each other, the solid melts.

6.7

FOCUS
Cause and effect, predictions

LEVEL
Elementary to intermediate

TIME
30 minutes

In Class

1 Read the text once at normal speed while students listen and think how they would represent it with the kind of chart shown in 4 below. Read the text again slowly and ask students to draw the chart. Read it at normal speed again so that students can make corrections.

2 Form pairs. Ask the students to use their diagrams to tell each other the original text. They should stay as close to the text as they can and remember its repetitive use of structure.

3 Bring the class together. Ask one student to say the first sentence in the chain and another the next. Continue round the class repeating the text two or three times and building up pace.

4 Write up *some* of the devices that English uses to make a cause and effect argument, e.g.

   a words or phrases that show a causal connection between a sentence and the one following:

   thus, therefore, so, in that case, consequently, as a consequence, as a result, and

   b Verb phrases of causation:

   this means that + noun/pronoun + verb

   this causes + noun/pronoun + *to* + verb

   the expansion results in + verb + *-ing*

   c Gerunds:

   'The steam expands, push*ing* up the piston.'

   d Putting sentences in time order:

   'The steam expands, pushing up the piston attached to a beam. The beam rises.'

5 Ask students to choose two stages from the dictated text and to practise linking them in every way they know.

6 Form pairs. Pairs use their diagrams of the text to produce a passage that excludes all the repetitive pattern practice of the original. Instead, they should use a variety of linking devices.

7 A student begins reading their text aloud then stops before the first linking device. You signal another student who continues with their own linkage then halts before the next. Continue, changing the linking device each time.

IN OUR COMPANY

Here, students draw up organisation charts and use them to describe where they work. They then use the same charts to analyse the kind of hierarchies that have developed in their class.

BEFORE CLASS

Prepare an organisation chart that is relevant to your students as in fig. 9. This could be of a small or large company, a school or university. It could also represent a legal, political or administrative system.

Beaconshire Grant Maintained Comprehensive School

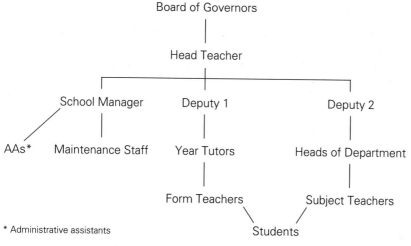

Fig. 9

6.8

FOCUS
Describing organisations

LEVEL
Lower intermediate to advanced

TIME
30 minutes

In Class

1 Sketch your chart on the board. A student describes it from the top down, saying something about *responsibility* and *function*, e.g.: *Under the head teacher are two deputies and a school manager. The school manager is responsible for the finances of the school and the maintenance of its building.* Another student repeats the description from the bottom up.

2 Ask how the organisation would cope with certain problems such as (for the above chart):
● minor disciplinary offences
● serious disciplinary offences
● changing a broken light bulb
● a student complaint about a bad subject teacher
● a severe blizzard

3 Students work alone and draw up an organisation chart showing the hierarchy and departmental structure of an organisation or company that they know well.

4 Call one student to the board to sketch and explain their chart.

5 Form pairs. Each pair selects the more complicated of their two charts then imagines that they have to fill *key* positions with other members of the class. They should give people the posts for which they think they are best suited. They can include you. If key posts remain unfilled, they can go outside the class to use fellow students.

6 Ask a pair to describe their organisation to the class. Suggest an appropriate problem, e.g. for a small company: 'a drunken lathe operator insults the workshop foreman'. Ask somebody in the pair to decide how the organisation could cope and how the people they have appointed would respond.

EXTENSION

7 Each student writes a letter to Sir/Madam describing their organisation chart.

8 Take in the letters then redistribute them. Each student tries to draw a chart of the organisation described.

9 Find out which students are struggling with garbled letters. Make the authors of these letters stop their work and come over to the students using them to explain what they have written and make it into a clear chart. After they have done so, make them go back and rewrite their letters, monitoring them closely.

CHAPTER 7

How it is and how it was

It is hard to imagine an ESP course that does not at some stage involve students in describing or defining events, places or things. For native speakers and foreign learners alike, study itself is a matter of grappling with new phenomena. These phenomena require definition and description. New devices require understanding and their parts need defining. The proof of our understanding of something often rests with our ability to describe it. In the EOP area also, schedules, business systems or plant will also have to be described.

The question of how things come about or what is happening at a given moment in time is a concern of business people, scientists and technologists everywhere. Description then cannot simply mean the process of locating and identifying the parts of a given phenomenon. Description must also state how those parts interact to produce change.

Activity 7.1 practises definitions. 7.2 and 7.3 develop the task of definition towards that of description by looking at what makes something what it is. 7.4 looks at how things are named and how acronyms are formed. 7.5 and 7.6 deal with the functions of different parts of technical systems. 7.7 deals with describing job functions through an unusual kind of interview. 7.8 focuses on specifications.

DIVORCED DEFINITIONS

An exercise to provide oral practice for students needing to define terms in any subject area.

BEFORE CLASS
1 Prepare two slips of paper for each student in the class: one slip with a definition, one with a term. Leave enough space for a sentence under the term. If necessary, reuse definitions and terms; you will also need six spare slips of paper, three with terms, three with definitions.
2 Draw up a list of relevant terms that students can define in twenty words or less, e.g. for legal English students:

injunction a court order that compels someone to stop doing something or not to do something.

Try to have at least as many terms as you have people in the class, though slightly fewer can work too.

7.1

FOCUS
Defining, understanding dictionaries

LEVEL
Lower to upper intermediate

TIME
20–30 minutes

EXTRAS
Slips of paper; a suitable specialist dictionary

3 Use a specialist dictionary. Write each term on one piece of paper and the definition on another. Leave enough space for a sentence under the term.

In Class

1 Give each student a term slip and its definition.
2 Tell students to exemplify each term by writing underneath it on the same slip in the space provided. They should add either an instance of 'action' or an example of a 'specification'.

e.g. *action*	**injunction**	for example, she got the court to forbid her ex-husband to come to her house
specification	**gas**	a substance such as hydrogen or oxygen

Write three spare exemplifications yourself for any three items then collect in the students' papers and make two piles of papers on your desk. One of definitions, one of terms and exemplifications.
3 Redistribute the definitions and exemplifications so that no student has ones that match.
4 Give students two to three minutes to memorise the definition they have just been given.
5 Take back the definitions. Tell students that they are a definition looking for an exemplification. To find their match they must move around the class introducing themselves in the following way: *A court order that compels someone to stop doing something or to do something*. They must also remember that everybody has an exemplification of something so each must be on the look-out for definitions wanting to link up with them without reason.
6 Exemplifications that find their matching definition wandering in the crowd should identify themselves. A definition person that is matched should take the exemplification slip then return it and the paired definition slip to the bottom of a pile on your desk. They should then select another definition slip from the top and a term slip that doesn't match and again set out in search of a match.
7 After most definitions have passed through most hands, bring the class back together.
8 Take in all slips. Invite a student to the board. Call out a term. Ask students to try to dictate a definition then the appropriate exemplification.

VARIATION
If you have a good supply of reference material or are dealing with terms that the class understand well, then get students to write their own definitions as well as the exemplifications. Proceed as from step 3 but be sure to correct the definitions before they are memorised.

WHAT MATTERS MOST

This is a way to increase awareness of the characteristics that make something what it is.

BEFORE CLASS

1 Prepare one piece of paper for each student with a relevant term written on it. Use the same terms more than once if necessary.
2 Think of four or more objects that relate to the students' area of study or interest, e.g. for lower level mechanical engineers: cylinder, piston, valve, crankshaft.
3 Write the terms down on pieces of paper, using each several times if necessary, so that you have one piece of paper for each student.

In Class

1 Form pairs. Give each pair a term for an object or process.
2 Write the following on the board:

CHARACTERISTICS

What it looks like   What it's made of   What it does

3 Ask the pairs to work out as many characteristics of their term as they can think of. They should use the headings on the board. Thus if their object is 'a piston' they might begin by writing: *it's cylindrical, made of metal alloy, turns the crankshaft.*
4 Ask the pairs to swap lists and objects.
5 Ask the pairs to either reduce the list of characteristics they have just been given to the few that are essential to define it or to add any that are missing. The definition must have enough characteristics to distinguish it from anything else.
6 Write the following on the board:

A _____ is that _____ which _____.

Ask each pair to formulate a definition by integrating their essential characteristics into this structure.

> e.g. *A piston is that part of the engine which is cylindrical, made of metal alloy and drives the crankshaft.*

7 One pair reads out their definition, but says *rabbit* in place of the thing that is being defined. The rest of the class try to challenge their definition by finding other ways to interpret it, e.g.

In the sentence: *A rabbit is that part of the engine which is cylindrical, is made of metal alloy and turns the crankshaft* the class could find grounds for interpreting 'a rabbit' as 'a piston rod'. If the class can only find one interpretation and this is the term the pair is working with, then say that the definition has survived the challenge.

8 Allow argument and repeat with other definitions.

7.2

FOCUS
Listing the characteristics of something

LEVEL
Elementary to upper intermediate

TIME
20 minutes

VARIATIONS

For English for medicine:

1 Decide on four diseases that the class know about or can find out about quickly.
2 Tell each student the name of a disease.
3 Write up: 'Symptoms', 'Where and Who', 'Causes'.
   Students write notes about the disease based on these headings. They can consult textbooks if necessary. They should not write down the name of the disease, e.g. Turner's Syndrome:

Where/Who: girls at puberty
Symptoms: no secondary sexual characteristics at puberty, stunted growth, possible amenorrhoea, webbing of the neck, cubitus valgus and coarctation, possible mental retardation, oedema of the extremities and loose neck folds at birth
Causes: a few 45XO sex chromosomes are XO/XX with positive sex chromatin 1

(Catzel, 1984, p. 207)

4 Students swap notes with somebody who has a different disease.
5 Each student uses the notes to write a coherent paragraph about the disease that begins with the name of the disease and continues: _____ *occurs among* _____. If they cannot think of the name of the disease, they leave the first part blank and write the paragraph.
6 Students read paragraphs to each other and ask for help in completing blanks.

7.3   ASPECTS OF AI

FOCUS
Describing and
defining thought/
intelligence

The topics of defining and describing interrelate. A way to define one item may be to describe it in a way that makes it distinct from any other. Here, the item is *thought* itself.

In Class

LEVEL
Upper
intermediate to
advanced

1 Write the following on the board:

Thought is the process   which
                           whereby
                           where

TIME
30 minutes

2 Brainstorm ways to complete this statement. Write possible completions on the board. In order to get more suggestions, show how the completions might be inadequate. Do not worry about correct English at this stage.
3 Ask each student to write down an economical definition of *thought* on a scrap of paper. Circulate and correct the English over their shoulders.

4 Tell students that they have to design a machine that can think like a human being. Form groups of four, each with a secretary to write down ideas while the group suggests what thinking like a human involves. Circulate and feed the following questions into groups where the going is slow or a solution found too easily:
- Can we think without language?
- What is the relationship between thought and creativity?
- What is the relationship between joking and thinking?
- Do our thoughts determine how we see or vice versa?
- Is thought rational?
- Can animals think?
- If other animals can think, how do human and animal thought differ?

5 After a few minutes bring the class back together. Select a student, borrow their definition, read it out, then tell the class that you are an intelligent machine. You cannot do more or less than what the definition implies. Get the class to ask questions in order to find out whether you can do what you should be able to do. Then let the class decide whether your answers fit the definition, e.g.:

Definition: Thought is the process whereby we own the world.
Student A: Can you dream?
Teacher: Yes.
Student B: Dreaming and owning the world are not the same.
Teacher: But I can think without dreaming.
Student C: No.

6 Select a student to role play their own definition and to fend off class questions in a similar fashion. Repeat with other students.

EXTENSION
7 Students write a paragraph on the topic 'What does *thinking* mean?'

ODD ACRONYMS

In English, a specialisation will often build its terminology with several noun adjectives modifying a head noun.

e.g.   Inertia   reel   seat   belt

       (noun)   (noun)   (noun)   (head noun)

In many languages this is not possible and so your students may find it useful to practise building such constructions. Here, the practice is based on inventing and interpreting acronyms.

BEFORE CLASS
Invent a technical term which is or which includes a noun adjective. You can use as many noun adjectives as you choose, either by them-

7.4

FOCUS
Building technical terms, using acronyms and noun adjectives

LEVEL
Lower intermediate to advanced

TIME
30 minutes

selves or in combination with other adjectives or verb participles. Make up an acronym for your term and decide on a meaning.

e.g.   MACM = music   assisted   coffee   maker

(noun)   (verb participle)   (noun) $\left(\begin{array}{c}\text{head}\\\text{noun}\end{array}\right)$

a device based on the astonishing discovery that the taste of coffee is improved when it is made to music.

In Class

1 Think of three terms that use nouns as adjectives. Write only their acronyms on the board. These terms can be generally known by their acronyms or not. For example:
ABC (activity based costing), NATO – generally known; IRSB (inertia reel seat belt) – not generally known.

2 Ask students to say what the acronyms stand for and write them up on the board as they do. If an acronym gives trouble, write up one of the words it stands for. Ask for more suggestions. Continue with other words if necessary.

3 Point out how these terms use nouns as adjectives.

e.g.   North   Atlantic   Treaty   Organisation

(adjective)   (noun)   (noun) $\left(\begin{array}{c}\text{head}\\\text{noun}\end{array}\right)$

4 Ask students to think of devices they would like to invent in order to improve their home, car or workplace and to give these devices names that include noun adjectives. They can use dictionaries if they like.

5 Call a student to the front of the class and ask them to write the acronym of their device vertically on the board, then to explain what the device does without saying what it's called.

6 After the explanation, the class try to work out what the acronym stands for.

e.g.   A student suggests: *music and coffee machine.*
The student at the board writes: M   music
A
C   coffee
M

They continue until they get all the words.

7 Repeat with other students and other acronyms.

VARIATION
At step 4, ask students to think of a political, social, scientific, academic or professional movement they would like to found. The name must use one or more noun adjectives.

WHAT DOES IT DO?

Things are often described and items sometimes even defined through their function. This exercise asks students to question the function and purpose of the familiar.

In Class

1 Say the following sentence: *It's for getting from one place to another.* Write it on the board.

2 Form pairs. Each pair lists as many devices that have this 'function' as they can think of in one minute.

3 Call time and ask a student to tell you the first item on their list. Write it on the board: e.g. *car*

4 Ask another student for another different item (e.g. *train*) and write this up too.

5 For each word, ask students to try to refine your original sentence so that it can show that the two devices have different functions, e.g.:

Car: It's for getting from one location to another by road.

Train: It's for getting from town to town by the straightest route.

6 Ask a student to give you another object from their list that could have the same function as one of the two just written up, e.g.:

Bicycle: It's for getting from one location to another by road.

7 Ask a student to redefine the function of either of the objects now at issue so as to distinguish it from the other, e.g.:

Bicycle: It's for getting from one place to another by road without damaging the environment, and using human propulsion.

Car: It's for getting one or more people from one place to another by road using a petrol-driven motor as propulsion.

8 Ask again for other objects to which the definitions could apply.

EXTENSION

9 Students state the function of any device that is relevant to their specialisation. The class try to guess what the device is. If they are wrong, the student expands on the function. The class guess again etc.

7.5

FOCUS
Describing the functions of things

LEVEL
Elementary to upper intermediate

TIME
15–20 minutes

7.6

FOCUS
Describing the
functions of
things, describing
systems

LEVEL
Elementary to
upper
intermediate

TIME
20–30 minutes

EXTRAS
Slips of paper

UNNAMED PARTS

Here, students assemble systems from parts which they name by their function. The exercise, for classes of less than twenty, is written for Technical English, but scientific and commercial versions exist.

BEFORE CLASS

Decide on two or more similar technical systems to be assembled, different engine systems for example; (electric, petrol, diesel, jet and steam). List the main parts of the systems. The more advanced your students are in English and their specialisation, the more parts you can list.

In Class

1 Form pairs. Assign each pair a system. Different pairs can have the same system.
2 Tell them that they are racing each other to assemble their system. They will do this by asking you for parts. Say that you are an ignorant English teacher so that the names of the parts mean nothing. They will only get a part when they tell you its function and not its name. Warn them to be as precise about function as possible. For example, they should try to distinguish the corresponding parts, e.g. the functions of petrol engine and diesel engine pistons.
3 Each pair tries to list the parts they will need and the function of each.
4 Each pair in turn asks you for a part, which they can't name but have to describe in terms of their function. If they get the function correct, you write the name of the part and of its system on a slip of paper and give it to them: e.g. piston – diesel engine. If a pair is inaccurate, give them nothing. If they are ambiguous, give them the wrong part, e.g.:

student   the part that is driven down by the combustion of the fuel/air mixture

teacher   (gives them a slip saying 'diesel engine piston' when they know that a petrol one is wanted)

If students ask for a part that shows they are breaking the system down into too many components, (e.g. head gasket) simply tell them: *Not necessary,* and ask them to try again. They will quickly understand the level of detail required.

5 You continue until a pair think they have enough parts to complete their system. This pair describes what they have assembled. If their system is incomplete according to your list, then tell them the name of a missing part by pointing out how the system would be defective, e.g. *When your piston is driven down it can't come up again.*; or by simply asking about the part directly: e.g. *What about the piston rod?* When a pair have got everything, get them to help others complete their inventories.

VARIATIONS

1 For elementary students: refer to very simple objects such as tables, chairs etc.
2 For science students: give them the name of two or more experiments and ask them to assemble the necessary apparatus by describing the function of each part.
3 For commercial English students: ask them to put together the organisation of a company, describing the personnel by function not job title.

SO WHAT DID I DO?

7.7

I once had the peculiar experience of being interviewed for a job that I had not applied for. Even stranger was the fact that I went through the interview without knowing what the job was. My reaction was to think: 'This must be something important so I had better make a good impression.' I simply answered the questions and tried to work out what the job was from what was being asked. I didn't come away with a job, but I did get an idea for a teaching activity. It goes like this.

Humans have functions just as machines do. Here, the human looks back and describes the function that they never knew they had.

BEFORE CLASS

Prepare a copy of a different job advert for every three or four students. The adverts should detail a substantial list of the qualities, qualifications and types of experience required.

In Class

1 Divide the class into groups of three or four, give each group a different advertisement and ask them to study secretly.
2 Divide the class into interviewing panels of three or four. Allot one candidate to each panel. Tell the panels to interview their candidate for the job for five minutes without ever letting on what the post is. Panels should find out as much about the suitability of the candidate as they can while divulging as little about the job as possible. Candidates cannot ask what the job is. Panels should skip the part of an interview where the candidate asks questions.
3 After about five minutes, the candidates exchange places with one member of the panels and you redistribute the job advertisements. The interviews then begin again.
4 Repeat step 3 until each student has been a candidate.
5 Tell the students that they got the job they applied for and have had it for a number of years. Now they are writing the employment section of their CV and must state what the job was and what they did. They must do this by using the information gleaned from the

FOCUS
Interviewing, describing job functions, writing CVs

LEVEL
Upper intermediate to advanced

TIME
40 minutes

EXTRAS
Copies of job ads

interviews, inventing what they do not know. Ask them to use the following headings:

Position   Employer   Function   Dates

6 Circulate the advertisements and see if students can recognise the jobs they were interviewed for. Ask them to look for the similarities between the candidate profiles and what they put in their CVs.

EXTENSION

7 Students rewrite or correct their job descriptions. Correct over their shoulders, concentrating on language not content.
8 Circulate the advertisements. Ask students to write another description to fit another advertisement, thus extending the employment part of their CV.

RATIONALE

Job interview role plays cover important ground but rarely work well. This is because the students know there is nothing at stake apart from some English practice. In this case both candidates and panels have things they must and must not do. The interview is a battle of wits rather than a 'let's pretend' situation. It also provides a useful springboard for practice in job descriptions.

7.8   SPECIFICATIONS

FOCUS
Listing specifications, describing a system

LEVEL
Intermediate to advanced

TIME
40 minutes

This is a simple way to get students listing and discussing the specifications of a piece of equipment to help them do what is difficult or impossible.

In Class

1 Students think of being able to do something that is impossible with today's technology but which they desire. Students must be able to express the desired thing in one or very few words, e.g. *fly, disappear, levitate, learn English instantly.*
2 Form two groups. Each group takes a few minutes to select the wish that is most attractive to all of them. They should discuss all the proposals then vote, with nobody voting for their own idea.
3 Each group decides on the name and specifications of the machine that could help them do what they cannot, e.g. If the desire was *fly*, you might get as a start:

Personal Flight Machine
1 Portable.
2 Compact, can be put away in a space of half a cubic metre.
3 Low energy consumption.
4 Rapid enough to compete with current ground transportation systems.
etc.

4 Each group tells the specifications to the other.

EXTENSION

5 Each group swaps specifications then tries to sketch a diagram of a machine that meets the ones they have been given. They can resort to science fiction as well as to science but must make the design sound convincing.

6 Each group explains their design to the other, inviting questions and criticism.

CHAPTER 8

Reasoning it out

This chapter helps students to talk about cause and effect and to argue logically in English. 8.1 is more a set of procedures based on the idea of trying to reason out what would happen to the environment if certain variables were changed. The scope for this kind of activity is almost unlimited. Do not hesitate to write your own versions. 8.2 uses the old parlour game of 'Consequences' to give practice in reasoning in almost any specialisation. 8.3 is based on a classical technique for improving logical argument. In 8.4 students explore cause and effect by working out what would happen to life in a two-dimensional universe. 8.5 introduces the language of diagnosis by getting the class to construct a simplified 'expert system'. 8.6 turns to experiment design, using as an example the theory of 'Morphic Resonance'.

8.1

FOCUS
Talking about cause and effect

LEVEL
Lower intermediate to advanced

TIME
30–40 minutes

PLAYING WITH VARIABLES

Here, students have to reason out exactly what happens to the system as a whole when one of its variables is changed.

In Class

1 Write *climate* at the top of the board. Elicit the components of climate. Write them up, attaching them to the system in order to make an organisation chart (fig. 10). If there is a subsystem such as 'the atmosphere', elicit key components (*nitrogen*, *oxygen* etc.). If you think something important has been missed, draw a box with a question mark in it.

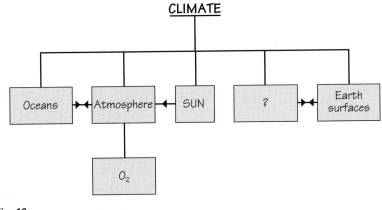

Fig. 10

2 Split the class into groups of four to five. Assign each group a different component of the system without telling other groups what it is. Ask each group to treat their component as a variable in what follows, e.g.:

Group 1 = *carbon dioxide*
Group 2 = *the moon,* etc.

3 Ask each group to put their heads together and to think what happens to their system when their variable is tampered with, e.g. if the carbon dioxide proportion of the atmosphere increases. Obviously, tampering with a variable like the moon, (e.g. the moon drifts off into space) will need considerable creative thought from a group since this is not a much debated or very plausible scenario. The moon drifting off can be interesting, however, if you encourage students to consider such issues as the relationship of climate to tides.

4 Ask each group to think how their system is working a century after the change in the variable. For example, depending on the theory adopted, they might decide that there is an ice age or that low-lying land floods and the seas rise.

5 After about ten minutes, each group recounts their changed scenario to the class, but without mentioning the variable. The rest of the class try to reason back and guess the variable that has been altered. For example, someone might guess: *I think a rise in carbon dioxide precipitated global warming resulting in a higher snowfall in the Arctic and the movement of glaciers from the poles.*

VARIATIONS
a Ecosystem
1 Put this simple model of the ecosystem on the board.

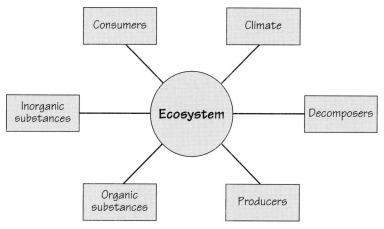

Fig. 11

2 Ask a student who feels confident to try to explain it to the class. Take a back seat and become a quiet student in your own class.

3 When you feel that the model has been understood, form groups of three or four and ask each group to change the way one of the components of the system interacts with the rest:

Consumers are self-consuming. They do not depend on producers.
or:
The ozone layer is depleted. It no longer filters sunlight.

4 Proceed as from step 3 in the basic procedure.

b Evolution

1 Ask students to imagine the planet in a natural state before the advent of man.
2 Ask them to help you invent an animal. Get details of:
   ● class (mammal, reptile etc.)
   ● locomotion (walking upright, flying, swimming)
   ● habitat
   ● gestation/breeding habits
   ● feeding habits
   ● size/appearance
   Ask an artistic student to try to draw a picture on the board.
3 Form groups of three to four.
4 Declare a gradual change in the environment of the animal, e.g. *a more variable climate (hotter summers and colder winters)* or *the arrival of another larger consumer of the same food sources.* Give the groups two minutes to discuss how the animal will adapt in order to survive. They can alter any of the characteristics of the animal. Survival is mandatory.
5 Every five minutes mention a new change that affects your species of animal. The groups discuss changes to the animal. Mention at least five changes.
6 Ask a group to draw the animal that has evolved. In turn, each group reports on its animal to the class.

c Physics

Suggest the cancellation of a well-known law of physics, e.g. When a solid is heated, it expands. Ask students to speculate on what would happen.

CAUSAL CONSEQUENCES

This activity is based on the old parlour game of 'Consequences'. It will work in almost any specialisation.

BEFORE CLASS

1 Think of at least five relevant theories. The ideal number would be one per student, but you can use the same one for different class members. These could be very general theories that contradict what is known: The earth is flat.;
or express a simple truth: The earth goes round the sun.;
or which direct the class more closely towards a specific science: Two ions with opposite charges will attract one another.;
or to different areas of study from their own:
A man is innocent until proven guilty.
Alternatively, use different types in combination.
2 Write each theory at the top of a blank sheet of paper. Continue until you have one sheet of paper for each student.

In Class

1 Hand out the papers and get the students into as near a circle as possible.
2 Ask each student to read the theory at the top of the paper then fold over their paper and cover it up.
3 Ask each student to write a statement expressing something that they think follows from the theory.

e.g.   The world is flat.
Therefore, if you go far enough you will fall off.

Two ions with opposite charges will attract one another
thus forming an ionic bond.

Note that the second example forms one sentence with the first statement. This is to be encouraged. Students use coherence markers and linkers and adjust their punctuation to achieve this. However, they must write on the line below the phrase they have been given.

4 Ask each student to pass their paper to their right-hand neighbour with the top folded down.
5 Insist that each student reads only what they can see on the paper they receive from the left. That is, they are not allowed to unfold the flap at the top which hides what had been written before. Encourage them to use different connective devices.

e.g.   *Therefore if you go far you will fall off.*
Which is why people travel rarely.

Ask the students to fold their paper again so that only what they have just written can be seen.
6 Repeat steps 4 and 5 several times.

FOCUS
Logical argument

LEVEL
Lower to upper intermediate

TIME
15–30 minutes

EXTRAS
A class set of papers with a theory written at the top

7 One student reads the last sentence on their paper first then sees if the class can guess what the original notion or theory was. If they cannot, the student unfolds the next consequence, reads it and lets the class guess again, and so on. Students who recognise the paper as their original one, should not reveal the theory.

EXTENSION

8 Redistribute the consequence chains. Ask each student to use theirs as the basis of a paper that states the consequences of a new theory.

e.g. *Hardy and Shrine established that the world was flat in 1994. This had profound consequences in the field of travel as it was appreciated that a navigational error could result in a traveller falling off the world. The result of this realisation . . .*

VARIATIONS

a Prevention and enablement

1 Think of at least five imaginary events that prevented or enabled something and which could have yet larger consequences.

e.g. ● The discovery of oil under Windsor Castle . . .
● The planting of trees in the Hawkura valley . . .
● The building of a dam in the Nile delta . . .

Write each such statement on the top of a sheet as above.

2 Write phrases of prevention and enablement on the board:

e.g. *allowed/permitted/enabled* + (noun) + (*to*)
meant they could/could not   made possible/impossible
prevented + (noun) + (*from . . . -ing*)

3 Ask students to suggest examples showing how these can be used: *The planting of trees enabled villagers to gather firewood quickly and efficiently.*

4 Give out the papers and go on from step 1 in the basic procedure.

8.3

FOCUS
Expressing
deductive
argument

LEVEL
Intermediate to
advanced

TIME
20 minutes

SOCRATES IS A MAN

This is an exercise that gives quick oral practice in logical argument.

In Class

1 Make sure that students understand deductive as opposed to inductive argument. Explain how in a deductive argument the truth of one proposition follows from the one before it. The argument is not empirical; it doesn't reach out into the world to justify itself. Give the following classic example:

All men are mortal.
Socrates is a man.
Therefore Socrates is mortal.

2 Elicit adjuncts or linking phrases that show one statement to be a consequence of another: e.g. *therefore, thus, then, so, if that is the case then, therefore/thus it follows that, as a result, as a consequence, consequently, hence, thereby.*

3 A student tries to continue the above argument, using one of the adjuncts: e.g. *so Socrates will die.*

4 Now treat the activity as a game. Repeat until students run out of ideas.

5 Make another statement: e.g. *Trees grow towards the sky.* The first student tries to deduce another statement from the first. If this student cannot do so within a few seconds, then eliminate them from the activity. If they make a statement that the class thinks does not logically follow, (e.g. *and trees are green*) the class call *foul*, and the student is out. Continue round the class.

6 Give your remaining core of students another statement. Continue until there is only one student remaining.

EXTENSION

For advanced and upper intermediates with a good academic background: discuss the role of deductive and inductive logic in science. This is a rich and fascinating area for those willing to enter it. Points for your students to consider:

a In order to be useful, deductive arguments must at some point be inductive. For example, 'all men are mortal' is an empirical truth. If a deductive argument includes no statement which has an empirical basis, it is tautological. That is, it refers only to itself.

b In science, the purest deductive argument will be expressed mathematically. However, a mathematical proof is only scientifically interesting if it is manipulating some part of reality, if it refers to the world outside itself. Otherwise you are moving into the domain of pure mathematics. Science explores reality, so its mathematical proofs begin and end in verbal statements about that reality.

c In science, empirical truths are established experimentally, that is, because the same thing happens each time we do something in a certain way, we assume it will always happen. Does this mean we have proved it to be true, or can we do no more than prove it isn't true? Some say that you cannot even falsify a proposition. Where does that leave science?

8.4

FOCUS
Linking causes
and effects

LEVEL
Intermediate to
advanced

TIME
40 minutes

THE TWO-DIMENSIONAL DOG

Here, students work together to deduce a series of consequences from a single proposition. This activity very much depends on students having an interest in ideas and being able to bring their own powers of reason to bear in a lesson. It is not for the intellectually idle.

In Class

1 Give students five minutes to consider what kind of an animal a dog would be if the universe had only two dimensions. They should draw the animal in such a universe.

2 Bring a student to the board to draw and explain their picture. Ask others to consider whether the student's animal is allowed by two dimensions. The most important conclusion they should come to is that the dog would fall apart since his digestive tract would be a space running from one end of his body to the other. The diagram would be as follows:

Fig. 12

Therefore, the animal would either need a different kind of digestive system or a new force to bind it together.

3 Form groups and ask them to list the features of life in a two dimensional universe. This new universe should be as close as possible to the one we know. How would creatures move without bumping into each other? Would congregation be possible? If your students are slow to come up with ideas, explain how people would be like 'pins' living inside squares, moving vertically as well as horizontally or hint at the possibility of meetings where people move outside their bodies.

4 Each group elects a spokesperson who explains their universe to the class. The class discuss and criticise. They should think particularly about whether everything suggested could happen in two dimensions.

ACKNOWLEDGEMENT
The idea of the two-dimensional dog comes from Hawking, S 1988, p.165.

SOLUTION SYSTEMS

This is a simple procedure that uses the idea of an 'expert system' to help students to introduce the language of diagnosis.

In Class

1 Write in large letters on the top of the board:

MY CAR WON'T START.

2 Ask the class what is the first thing they would look for. Formulate this as a question, e.g. *Does the ignition light come on?*
3 Ask the class to think of what they would look for if the answer is 'yes' and what if the answer is 'no'.

   e.g.   Yes
          Does the starter turn over?
   e.g.   No
          Is the battery completely flat?

4 Draw this as a primitive flow-chart. Do not worry too much about the details of flow-chart convention for this. Boxes and lines will do, e.g.;

5 Make sure students understand that each question must have a very limited number of possible answers. Two are best: e.g. *yes/no.* Three are possible, but more than four are unmanageable.
6 Form a 'yes' group and a 'no' group. Give each a large sheet of paper. The 'yes' group should develop the questions on their side and the 'no' group on theirs.

   e.g.   'Yes' group
          Does the starter just click or turn properly?

Allow each group to develop their parts of the chart in their different ways leading the person answering towards a 'cause'. Make sure they understand that the chart should not necessarily expand downwards but can also loop back. Different questions can lead to the same point.

8.5

FOCUS
Deducing causes
from effects

LEVEL
Lower
intermediate to
advanced

TIME
40 minutes

EXTRAS
Two poster-sized
sheets of paper

If they come to a cause or recommendation (e.g. *The battery's flat. Try recharging it*) they can point out of the chart with an arrow. Though they can carry the questioning almost as far as they want: e.g. *Does it take the charge?* etc.

EXTENSION

7 If one group finishes or starts to tire, bring the class together and spread one large sheet of paper on the floor or pin it up on the wall. Ask the two groups to redraw their parts of the system as one. This can be difficult and time consuming but is a useful discussion or negotiation exercise in itself.

8 Act the role of a system user. Say: *My car won't start.* Get the class to guide you through their chart to a cause or recommendation. Get a student who has been less involved in the activity to role play another system user. Prompt them to take a different route.

9 Ask students to use the complete chart to write a series of instructions about what to check if the car doesn't start.

VARIATIONS

This idea will work with almost any system that is malfunctioning, though to make it a plausible class activity some simplification may be necessary, e.g.:

a **Medicine:** *I have persistent headaches.* Then use students' expertise to help you ask for other examples.

b **Electricity:** *My fuse keeps blowing.*

c **Computing:** *The printer won't work.*

d **Business:** *The company's profits have fallen.*

8.6

MORPHIC RESONANCE: EXPERIMENT DESIGN

FOCUS
Experiment design

LEVEL
Intermediate to advanced

TIME
50–60 minutes

This activity is about finding the language to describe an experiment and to show how well it tests a given theory. It isn't just for science students since relating an experiment to the theory it is supposed to disprove involves skills of logical argument that are relevant to all disciplines. The activity was first designed for graduate EAP students and probably needs an informed input.

The theory of Morphic Resonance enjoyed some vogue in the 1980s. It held that something once learnt would then become easier for others to learn because our unseen environment was in some way remoulded and made more friendly to the new idea. It provided an explanation for how blue tits all over the world and without communication with each other suddenly knew how to open the milk bottles left on people's doorsteps at about the same time.

In Class

1 Explain the theory of Morphic Resonance.
2 Form groups of three or four and ask each to try to work out a practicable experiment that would disprove the theory.
3 If a group is stuck, suggest ideas along the lines of teaching something new to one isolated group in one part of the world then trying to teach it again a few years later to other groups in other parts of the world. Ask students to produce an idea even if they believe the theory cannot be falsified and is therefore unscientific. Tell any such students that they need an idea for later use.
4 Keep students in their groups then ask them to imagine that they have been given the opportunity to carry out their experiments. Say that they should write a rough report about the experiment under: *title, aims, apparatus/equipment/location* (as appropriate), *procedure, results, conclusions.* They can fabricate all evidence and draw conclusions accordingly. The conclusion should contain some statement about the validity of the theory.
5 When the groups have finished, ask one of them to read out their report then get the class to discuss whether the conclusion is really warranted by the results and the experiment itself. Has the theory really been tested? The problem with this kind of procedure is often the control of variables, e.g.

If some new technique was taught the first time in one month in a mountain village in the Yemen, then in three weeks in another village in Nepal, how do we know that the Nepalese were not more culturally disposed to it?

Students can criticise their own ideas.
6 Repeat with other groups.

RATIONALE
EST students need practice in expressing the relationship between an experiment and what it tries to prove. Morphic Resonance provides a useful route into this topic because the theory is at once both challenging for the experiment designer and accessible to all.

CHAPTER 9

Getting across

The activities that follow are for helping students to function better in seminars and meetings. They are not so much for showing students how to state a case as for helping them to impose themselves enough to be heard in the first place. Anybody who has had the experience of using a foreign language in a public or professional situation will know that entering a discussion is itself difficult. The livelier the debate, the more difficult the task of contributing to it, since you have to interrupt others' contributions in order to make your own. As you begin to speak, you feel you are walking out on to glass. The language of which you have such uncertain mastery may suddenly disintegrate and let you fall into embarrassment and confusion.

There is no room in this book to give the wider issues of confidence and assertion the treatment they need. Interested teachers could look at another title in this series, *The Confidence Book* (Davis and Rinvolucri, 1990). The following activities are more about language practice. 9.1 is a kind of experiment where students test their hypothesis about what makes a successful negotiator. In 9.2, students put together a personal interpretation of history using a tree metaphor, which acts as a structural outline of an essay. 9.3 exploits the technique of the scenario job interview where the interviewer puts the interviewee into situations that are likely to arise in the job they are applying for. 9.4 shows a way for students to find out about each others' interests and to explain their own. 9.5 helps students with the techniques of interrupting.

GETTING MY WAY

In this activity students try to find out more about the characteristics of a successful negotiator. There are two stages which can be done straight after each other, though it is better to have a break between them so that students do not directly connect the parts of the activity with each other.

The activity may seem best for commercial English students, but getting your way in argument is also a useful academic skill, while the theme of hypothesis and experiment applies to many specialisations.

In Class

STAGE 1

1 Tell the class to think about the characteristics of a successful negotiator. Write one characteristic on the board, leaving out the word in brackets: *I am (sensitive) to the needs of others.* Ask the class to try to fill in the blank. If they contribute ideas that are close to the word you have in mind or define other useful characteristics, then write these additional words around the space. If it is clear they are not going to guess the word, say their other ideas are not wrong, but that you are looking for *sensitive*.

2 Repeat with the sentences below and ask students to copy them down when the gaps have been filled.

I will (compromise) to solve problems when necessary.
I am committed to a (win/win) philosophy.
I have a high (tolerance) for conflict.
I am willing to (research) and (analyse) issues fully.
(Patience) is one of my strong points.
My tolerance for (stress) is high.
I am a good (listener).
Personal (attack) and (ridicule) do not bother me unduly.
I can identify (bottom-line issues) quickly.

3 Form A and B pairs. In order to assess the Bs' potential as negotiators, the As make questions from the statements they have written down. Bs should reply with a score out of ten, e.g.:

A: Is patience one of your strong points?
B: Hmm, 7

If the answer sounds out of character, the As should probe to get at the truth. Stress that it is more interesting if students are honest.

4 As and Bs swap roles. Collect the total scores for each student then write them on the board.

STAGE 2

5 Form two groups. Take group A aside and tell them that they have a three-year-old family saloon car that they want to sell. They have read that £4000 is the right price for this mileage and model. Take

9.1

FOCUS
Interviewing, negotiation, describing the characteristics of the negotiator

LEVEL
Lower intermediate to advanced

TIME
Stage 1: 30–40 minutes
Stage 2: 20 minutes

group B aside and tell them that they want to buy A's car for as little as possible. What A must not know is that B has come a long way to see the car and needs it quickly. Tell both groups that As have ten minutes to make a deal with Bs. They must make a deal otherwise they will score 0. The A student who sells for the highest price will be the A winner and the B who pays the least the B winner.

6 Form pairs of As and Bs and let them start their negotiations. Warn them one minute before time is up, then call stop.

7 See whether the winners of stage 1 were also the high scorers in stage 2. If they were not, discuss whether it was the first stage of the activity that was based on invalid premises or the second stage (the proof) that did not address these premises.

EXTENSION

8 Ask students to write a report under the subheadings, 'Aim', 'Method', 'Results', 'Conclusions'. Under 'Aim', they should say something like: *To test the theory that a good negotiator will have the following qualities.* Under 'Method' they describe how they used the class as a control group then gave them an activity where they had to haggle over the price of a car. The results should show whether there is any correlation between high and low scores in the two activities. You can use this as practice in drawing and interpreting graphs. The graph shows the scores from one of my classes on the characteristics assessment (stage 1) and the negotiation of a price. The negotiation scores were calculated by showing the price achieved as a percentage of 4000. No correlation between scores is apparent.

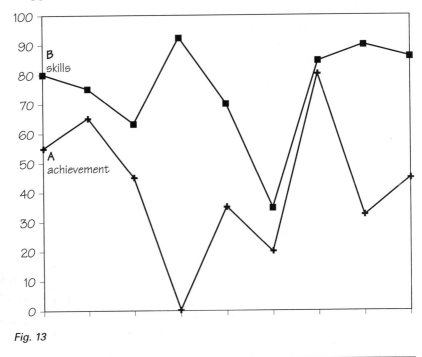

Fig. 13

Teachers or students with the knowledge can take this further and deal with issues of statistical significance.

ACKNOWLEDGEMENT
The list of sentences in step 2 are taken from Madox, 1988, p. 22.

HISTORY IS A TREE

This is an exercise in argumentation. The exercise is also a gentle and interesting way of raising cross-cultural issues for further discussion.

In Class

1 Tell your students that they will have to represent history as a tree. Tell them it can be any kind of tree they like. If they want to abstract into 'tree diagrams', they can. They can also think about trees in bloom or a group of different trees. They should label key parts of the tree to show what represents what.

2 Give them about ten minutes to work alone and draw their trees. Divide the board into six squares.

3 Look over the students' shoulders as they work and decide on the six trees that are most distinct from each other.

4 Ask one of the chosen six to present their tree to the class. They should do this by drawing their tree in one of the squares on the board and explaining how it means what it means. They should write their surname under the tree. The students should take notes, as if at a mini-lecture.

5 Ask the other five students to do the same while students take notes. When they have finished, there should be six trees on the board.

6 Ask each student in the class to work alone and to write a description of each tree in turn, saying how it means what it means. Stress that they should devote a paragraph to each tree and call them 'model 1, 2, 3' etc.

7 Ask them to write a concluding paragraph saying which tree they prefer and why.

8 Give the following dictation: *The Arborial Theory of History has been gaining widespread credence. There are basically six models: the (name of first presenter) _____ model, the _____ model, etc.*

9 Ask students to complete the dictation by writing what they have just done as if they were going to do it. Advise them to use the future simple, e.g. *I will first describe each model in turn then assess their respective merits and draw conclusions.*

10 The students now have a model essay with 'introduction–presentation–discussion and conclusions'. It does not matter if the introduction comes last, they can show where it goes with an

9.2

FOCUS
Argumentation, academic writing

LEVEL
Intermediate to advanced

TIME
60–90 minutes

arrow. Ask them to put their work on the wall or board so that everyone can circulate and examine each others' efforts and the presenters can see how well their models have been described.

11 Ask presenters for comments before you close.

RATIONALE

The tree metaphor is an excellent vehicle for eliciting different views of the same subject. I have not yet seen one model that was the same as another. Often the models reveal interesting cultural differences and these too can be discussed. The separateness of the models also encourages a proper theming of the essay.

9.3

FOCUS
Hypothesising, scenarios

LEVEL
Lower intermediate to advanced

TIME
50 minutes

EXTRAS
Class copies of one job advertisement with a detailed and varied job description

SCENARIO INTERVIEW

In a scenario job interview, the panel does not concentrate on finding out what the candidate has done but on what they *would* do in situations that are likely to arise if they take up the post. Here, students exploit the technique of scenario interviewing in order to practise language for coping with the unexpected in class and in life.

In Class

1 Form groups of three or four.
2 Explain what a scenario interview is. You can use the following example of a scenario.

You take up the position of personnel manager. You are resented by another employee who has been side-lined by your appointment. The employee is spreading bad feeling and damaging morale. He's efficient and we don't want to lose him. Imagine you call him into your office. What would you tell him?

3 Hand out the advertisement. Each group draws up one list of scenarios that they think appropriate for testing a candidate for this job. The list should include:
a The questions that they will put to the candidate.
b Reasons for including each of the scenarios, or a short explanation of how each relates to the job description.
Advise students to begin by speculating about what the candidate will actually do in the job on a day-to-day basis and the kind of problems that may arise.
4 After about ten minutes, ask the groups to tell you their suggested scenarios, explaining what they involve and how they relate to the job in question. Get the class to discuss how appropriate the scenarios are. If they consider a scenario useful, write the relevant interview questions on the board.
5 Ask a self-confident student to sit in front of the class. Call them the 'candidate'. Another student suggests a scenario. The 'candidate'

explains how they would react to this scenario. Repeat with the same candidate and another scenario.

6 Ask the 'candidate' to sit down. Ask them how well they answered the question and how good the question was. When they are finished ask the class for their opinion.

7 Repeat with one or two other candidates.

POSTER SESSIONS

Poster sessions at conferences are a way for people to find out about research topics that have a particular interest to them. The session is one where different participants put up 'posters' that are like advertisements for their current research. They get researchers talking to each other about topics of mutual interest. As an ESP activity, posters encourage concise summaries and help students to explain topics of academic or professional interest to each other.

In Class

STAGE 1

1 Ask students to select a topic that is of academic, professional or personal interest and which they think that others in the group may not know about.

> e.g.   For Doctors: A paper about a new kind of treatment
> For Business: Launching the CSC information management system

They can either go and read up on something new to them or organise their thoughts about something they already know. Academically advanced students can use their own research interests, the less knowledgeable can take some very well-known theory and treat it as if it were a discovery. Those who are good at bluffing can invent research in an area of interest.

2 Tell them to prepare a poster 'advertising' their topic. This should be a summary that can be taken in at a glance, something like a newspaper headline and beneath it a rubric to a non-existent article. There should be some attractive visuals, and care should be taken over layout and display. e.g.

For students with low academic knowledge:

GENERAL GAS LAW
The combination of the individual gas laws, Charles's Law (V = const) and Boyle's Law (V × T = const), has produced the General Gas Law

$$\left(\frac{P_1 V_1}{T_1} = \frac{P_2 V_2}{T_2}\right)$$

FOCUS
Explaining research interests

LEVEL
Lower intermediate to advanced

TIME
Stage 1: 15 minutes
Stage 2: 40 minutes

EXTRAS
A class set of poster-sized papers

STAGE 2

1 Ask students to rehearse presenting their posters. Go round the class correcting the posters. Ask students to rewrite them on the other side of the paper if necessary.

2 Form three groups, A, B and C. The As sit around the outside of the class displaying their posters. The Bs and Cs must find out about as many of the As' research topics as they can. They circulate from poster to poster and stop at one that catches their interest to ask for more information. No more than two students can stop at a given poster at one time.

3 When most of As' topics have been grasped, the As and Bs swap roles, then the Bs and Cs.

EXTENSION

4 Students write a short talk about any topic except their own.

5 They give the talk to the class as if to a conference.

ACKNOWLEDGEMENT

I learnt about Conference Poster Sessions from Celia Shalom (1993, p. 39).

9.5

FOCUS
Explaining a topic, interrupting and intervening

LEVEL
Lower intermediate to advanced

TIME
30 minutes

STUDENT TEACHER

In this activity students practise interrupting each others' micro lessons.

BEFORE CLASS

1 Check that students have mastered some interruption/intervention strategies that are appropriate for their place of study or work.

e.g. I am sorry, I don't get your point . . .
Excuse me, isn't it the case that . . .
Sorry, can you stop there a minute . . . etc.

2 Choose one or more topics in the students' subject specialisation, e.g. solving an equation, explaining a proof or theory or describing how an apparatus works.

3 Assign each topic to one student and ask them to prepare a small lesson about it. Say that they will be able to draw or write on the board. They can role play a teacher they know or be themselves.

In Class

1 Tell the class that they are going to hear a short talk. Their objective will be to interrupt the talk as often as possible. They do this by gesturing and then saying an 'interruption phrase' followed by a question. They should score every successful interruption in order to count up how many they have at the end. Explain that you are going to be chairperson. You will allow or disallow interrup-

tions. The student giving the talk will only deal with interruptions when you tell them to. Otherwise they will steam on regardless. Stress that interruptions should be well-mannered, sensible and correctly phrased, otherwise they will be ignored. They must interrupt by gesture first. They can only speak after you have acknowledged their gesture. (Students can also ask questions about answers to other questions.)

2 Tell the 'teacher' to begin the talk. Tell them to ignore the waving hands unless you signal them to stop. When you have signalled a stop, you will point to a student who wants to interrupt and they will speak. If their interruption is in correct English and fairly sensible, allow it, then tell the 'teacher' to reply. As far as possible, give everybody the same number of tries. The question of which interruptions to allow is very much one of personal judgement, but avoid too much repetition and too many requests for clarification of what is obviously comprehensible.

3 Students count up the interruptions to find who has had the largest number which have got a reply from the 'teacher'.

EXTENSION

4 Discuss whether the winner's success was due to:
   a a good command of interruption strategies;
   b where they were sitting;
   c an assertive character;
   d their sex;
   e some form of favouritism on your own part;
   f a good knowledge of the subject of the talk.

RATIONALE

You may feel that it would be better to give the talks yourself. The reasons for not doing this are:

● it is very difficult to talk and encourage people to interrupt you at the same time;

● students may be more reluctant to interrupt a teacher than a colleague;

● the 'student teacher' gets valuable practice in explanation and assertion.

Bibliography

Abdulazziz, M 1985 *The Computer Book, Programming and Language Skills for Students of ESL* Prentice Hall

Braudel, F 1979 *Le Temps Du Monde* Armand Collin

Brown, G 1983 *Discourse Analysis* CUP

Catzel, P 1984 *A Short Textbook of Paediatrics* Hodder and Stoughton

Coleman, H 1980 *Petroleum Upstream* Heinemann Science and Technical Readers

Coleman, H 1980 *Petroleum Downstream* Heinemann Science and Technical Readers

Collin, P 1986 *The English Law Dictionary* Peter Collin Publishing

Davis P and Rinvolucri, M 1988 *Dictation* CUP

Flowerdew, J 1993 An Educational, or Process, Approach to the Teaching of Professional Genres, *ELT Journal* 47/4/ October

Francis, D 1990 *Effective Problem Solving* Routledge

Hawking, S 1988 *A Brief History of Time* Bantam Press

Hutchinson, T 1988 *Making Materials Work in the ESP Classroom. Practice and Evaluation* Modern English Publications

Hutchinson, T and Waters, A 1987 *English For Specific Purposes, A Learning Centred Approach* CUP

Jordan, RR 1992 English for Academic Purposes (EAP), State of the Art Article *English for Special Purposes,* Vol 199X

Knott, G 1991 *Financial Management* Macmillan

Maley, A and Grellet, F 1981 *Mind Matters* CUP

Masters, P A 1986 *Science Medicine and Technology, English Grammar and Technical Writing* Prentice Hall

Mauranen, A 1993 Contrastive ESP Rhetoric, Metatext in Finnish English Economics Texts *English for Specific Purposes*, Vol 12

Moore, J 1979 *Discovering Discourse, Reading and Thinking in English* The British Council/OUP

Morgan, J and Rinvolucri, M 1986 *Vocabulary* OUP

Munby, J 1978 *Communicative Syllabus Design* CUP

Robinson, P 1991 *ESP Today: A Practitioner's Guide* Prentice Hall International

Shalom, C 1993 Established and Evolving Spoken Research Process Genres, Plenary Lecture and Poster Sessions, Discussions at Academic Conferences *English for Special Purposes* Vol 12

Stone, B 1993 *Physics GCSE Passbook* BPP Letts Educational Ltd

Swales, JM 1990 *Genre Analysis* CUP

Wilson, J 1986 *ELT Documents 123: General Principles, ESP for The University* Pergamon Press

Woodward, T 1991 *Models and Metaphors in Language Teacher Training, Loop Input and Other Strategies* CUP

Language Through Literature

Susan Bassnett and Peter Grundy

This book has over a hundred ideas for teachers on how to use poetry and short stories. Suitable for teenagers and adults with activities for beginners as well as more advanced learners, it stimulates students to write literary texts and poetry as well as helping to develop reading skills.

ISBN 0582 07003 1

Musical Openings

David Cranmer and Clement Laroy

Musical Openings offers a refreshing approach to language learning by showing how music can inspire student creativity and enthusiasm. Accompanied by a music cassette, the activities stimulate students of all levels to communicate meaningfully in speech and writing. Covering all aspects of language study, the book demonstrates how music can create a positive learning environment for both teenagers and adults.

ISBN 0582 07504 1

Ways Of Training

Tessa Woodward

Anyone interested in teacher training: trainers, trainees or course organisers, will find this book ideal. Clearly and intelligently presented, it covers a range of topics from planning, observing and discussing teaching to reducing stress.

ISBN 0582 06493 7

The Pronunciation Book

Tim Bowen and Jonathan Marks

All areas of pronunciation from individual sounds and stress to intonation are covered in this book. It is an invaluable guide to the teaching of pronunciation to students of all levels and nationalities.

ISBN 0582 06491 0

For further information on Pilgrims Longman Resource Books and other materials for language teachers published by Longman ELT, contact your local Longman representative or agent, or write to:

Longman ELT
Longman Group Ltd,
Edinburgh Gate,
Harlow,
Essex
CM20 2JE

Teaching Teenagers

Herbert Puchta and Michael Schratz

This book provides a wealth of imaginative and practical techniques. Especially useful for state school foreign language teachers, it gives useful insights on how and when to use the students' mother tongue; how to develop social skills and how to lay the foundations of good discipline. There are chapters on teaching grammar and literature and a useful section on computer assisted language learning.

ISBN 0582 03763 8

Creative Grammar Practice

Günter Gerngross and Herbert Puchta

Ideal for adults and teenagers, this book makes communicative grammar teaching feasible even in large classes. The emphasis is on helping students to correct grammatical forms using a variety of creative techniques. This book really encourages students to remember what they have learnt about grammar.

ISBN 0582 08957 3

The Confidence Book

Paul Davis and Mario Rinvolucri

This book shows teachers how to help students to become more cooperative learners. The activities are designed to improve students self-image and confidence. It is especially suitable for intensive multilingual beginner and elementary courses. In addition, there is a useful exam preparation chapter which makes it suitable for use at higher levels.

ISBN 0582 03766 2

The Recipe Book

Seth Lindstromberg

The Recipe Book is a portable kit of ready-to-use activities for all levels including advanced. Its nine chapters include a wide range of activities which focus on accuracy, teaching vocabulary, story telling, role plays and using pictures.

ISBN 0582 03764 6

Talking Texts

Randal Holme

This book offers more than 60 ideas for encouraging students to read for meaning and then to use, present or criticise what they've learnt. It provides ideal material to stretch well-motivated upper-elementary and intermediate students. An excellent resource for teachers of general English as well as English for Academic Purposes.

ISBN 0582 07002 3

Headstarts

Natalie Hess

100 activities are presented to motivate students to read assigned texts such as short stories, poems and articles in this book. It also helps them to gain a better understanding when they read. It is especially useful for teachers of foreign (and native!) languages in state schools.

ISBN 0582 06492 9

Lessons from the Learner

Sheelagh Deller

This book illustrates a new approach to lesson planning. There are suggestions on how to enhance the coursebook as well as tailoring lessons to the students interests and level. The result is lessons which are useful and fun as well as easy to plan with few resources and little preparation time.

ISBN 0582 07004 X

Alternatives

Richard and Marjorie Baudains

Fun and easy to use, this book is full of games, new ways to learn grammar and suggestions on ways to stimulate conversation. Suitable for all levels, it can be used in a variety of teaching situations, and is an ideal complement to the main coursebook in use.

ISBN 0582 03767 0

Visual Impact

David A Hill

This versatile book uses pictures to add meaning to grammar, stimulate oral work and help students to enjoy creative writing. Useful at all levels, it also provides tips on how to build up your own working bank of visuals for use again and again.

ISBN 0582 03765 4

Creative Questions

Natalie Hess and Laurel Pollard

Creative Questions offers a variety of lively activities to practise the interrogative in class. Whether you are teaching grammar, fluency, reading or writing, this book will provide inspiration. As well as being suitable for all levels and abilities, many of the activities require little or no preparation. Student centred activities emphasise production of language and natural communication between students.

ISBN 0582 08958 1

Business English Recipes

Judy Irigoin and Bonnie Tsai

Business English Recipes is a photocopiable resource ideal for all business-orientated English courses. Creative in their approach, the activities are original and use photocopiable worksheets, authentic business documents and problem solving games and simulations to develop students' ability to use English in everyday business situations. The activities can be adapted for one-to-one teaching as well as for different professions, countries and cultures.

ISBN 0582 08960 3

Planning from Lesson to Lesson

Tessa Woodward and Seth Lindstromberg

This book offers a refreshing approach to lesson planning which will save you time and energy before lessons. It also provides the experienced teacher with alternative ideas and techniques. In addition to a clear introduction, the book is a rich source of sound practical advice for teachers. There are activities for use with mixed ability classes too.

ISBN 0582 08959 X